In Pakistan

JOURNEYS IN THE LAND BEYOND THE HEADLINES

JAMES B. SHUMAN

ISBN: 0615881173
ISBN 13: 9780615881171

Requests for permission to make copies of any part of the work should be submitted online at jbshuman@aol.com/ or mailed to the following address:

Markhor Press
Permissions Department
2513 Preakness Court
Santa Rosa, CA 95401

This book is dedicated to my beloved wife, Elfie.
She came, she saw, she conquered.

The Beginning

"Pakistan?" Elfie asked. "Pakistan?" She shook her head. "You've got to be kidding. With terrorists blowing everything up and the government about to fall?"

I was surprised. When we had married a few years before, I had been impressed by her passion for travel and her wide-ranging curiosity. She loved new experiences.

"Don't worry," I said. "We'll be safe."

"That's not what I've read," she said. "why go now ...?" We were at breakfast and she put down her coffee cup and turned toward our garden, verdant in the brilliant Southern California sunshine.

"Because I want to write a book about Pakistan. I think people should know that Pakistan is more than jihadist terrorists. It has another side, where people are living normal lives, marrying, raising families, enjoying life. I know Pakistan well. I've seen aspects of it that you seldom read about. It's far more than the newspaper or television stories of bombings and poverty. It's complex. It's interesting. And it's important. It's going to be in the news for a long time."

"But why now?" she asked again. It was September of 2007, and newspapers were full of stories about Pakistan's instability and dangers.

"I want to go now because someday the Pakistan I know, the normal, human country, may be only a memory, the shattered remnants of a failed attempt to build a model nation. That's the other part of my fascination: Pakistan was created in an attempt to build a model nation. It shares something unique with the United States. It was established as a religious state, as were formative parts of the U.S., particularly Pennsylvania and Massachusetts. I wonder how it is managing. Most reports tell only the negatives: crumbling infrastructure, deteriorating roads, decrepit railways, terrorist attacks, political corruption, the gap between the rich and the poor, and so on. I want to show the little known side of Pakistan, the parts that work, the hospitable people, the fascinating history. I'd like to have you with me. I think you'll like Pakistan."

"What did you like best?" she asked.

I thought for a moment. "Each time has been different. When I first went to Pakistan in 1969, it was peaceful, slow moving and tranquil. It seemed like the land, the India, Rudyard Kipling wrote about. In many ways, it seemed not to have changed, and I was fascinated by the contrasts. The cities, Karachi, Lahore, Islamabad, were relatively modern. The villages were like illustrations from a book of Bible stories. In one village, which I remember vividly, women were clustered around a community well drawing water with canvas bags and camels were standing patiently nearby on the hot desert sand. On later visits, I saw the building of an infrastructure, roads and, the biggest of all, the Indus Waters Project which included the giant Mangla Dam south of Lahore and Tarbella, south of Islamabad, with broad link canals reaching out to irrigate the parched countryside. And I felt the growing tension when Russia invaded Afghanistan.

"There were more personal memories, too: my delight in the warmth of the people, who accepted me not as a visitor but as a friend; of being taken to wild and rugged polo matches at the world's highest polo field in the remote Hindu Kush mountains; of trout fishing in pristine mountain lakes, using bread dough for bait; of a long summer's evening dinner party full of warm and interesting conversation; of traveling on the spectacular and landslide-prone Karakoram Highway as it climbed between the world's highest mountains and the deep gorge of the Indus River; of watching a village Bityan, a shaman, dance while sucking blood from the severed head of a freshly-killed goat; of giving a talk to a group of beautifully-dressed women from isolated farming villages who were learning to earn their own money raising chickens."

I paused for breath. "There are so many rich memories accumulated over thirty years," I added.

I knew my experiences couldn't be repeated, but I wanted Elfie to share new ones. There was another reason, too. We were on the American advisory board of a school for Afghan refugee girls outside Peshawar. I thought we should visit it.

But I hadn't answered her most important question.

She leaned forward and looked at me, still disturbed. "What about the terrorists?" she asked. "The Taliban? Al Qaeda? Will we be safe?"

"Danger is there," I answered. "Pakistan is a nation on the edge, teetering between stability and chaos. It could go either way. But, if we stay out of crowds, we'll be safe."

She looked at me doubtfully.

"You'll like Pakistan," I said.

"I'm not sure," she said.

"Let's ask Saeed," I said. Saeed Anwar Khan was a long-time friend. He lives in Rawalpindi, and he had offered to help make appointments for me if we came.

"Jim will be busy with meetings and interviews," Elfie wrote in an e-mail. "I don't know the customs of your country. Will I, as a woman, have to sit in a hotel room and wait, or will I be able to move around freely, visit other women with children, or even accompany Jim?"

His answer came an hour or so later.

"I think you should come to Pakistan," he replied. "I am sure you will like Pakistan, you will like Jim's friends and we assure you to make your trip comfortable and memorable. You can accompany Jim during the meetings if you wish so – otherwise we will arrange different things for you. You will meet families of all of Jim's friends and my friends. My daughter will take you around to museums and other interesting places. I am sure you will have a good time."

I printed it out. Elfie read it. Her face relaxed.

"Okay," she said with a big smile. "That's it. I'm coming."

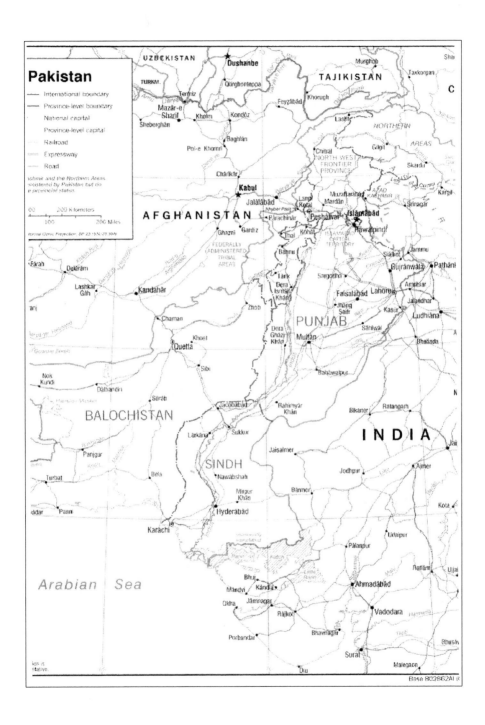

Pakistan

- —— International boundary
- —— Province-level boundary
- ⬩ National capital
- ⬩ Province-level capital
- —— Railroad
- ▭▭▭ Expressway
- —— Road

*ashmir and the Northern Areas
administered by Pakistan but do
ie provincial status.*

| 00 | 200 Kilometers |
| 100 | 200 Miles |

normal Conic Projection, SP: 23:19 N / 29:30 N

1

We decided to walk across the border.

For more than six decades, this invisible line has separated India and Pakistan. It runs some 2, 000 miles from the salty wastes of the Rann of Kutch on the Arabian Sea north through the scorching deserts of Sindh to the bitterly cold, snow-covered heights of the Karakoram Mountains at the Chinese border. Legally, you can cross it on foot in only one place: through heavily guarded gates near a village called Wagah, in the Punjab between Amritsar in India and Lahore in Pakistan.

Once, the border did not separate the two nations. It separated two very similar provinces of India: East Punjab and West Punjab. In 1947, it was the site of inhuman horror. The British, after ruling India for more than 200 years, had given the South Asian subcontinent independence. Hastily, with little more care than if they had used only a pencil and an Ordnance Survey of India road map, they had split India into two nations: Hindu India and Muslim Pakistan. Pakistan itself was divided into two separate areas, one in the western part of India, called West Pakistan, the other a thousand miles to the northeast, called East Pakistan.

The new borders separated not only nations, but also communities, friends, families. In the west, ten million people, maybe more, streamed across the dividing line. Hindus and Sikhs fled east to the sanctuary of India. Muslims fled west to establish an ill-defined new nation. Endless lines of people, glum faced, fearful, uncertain of their future, passed each other in single file. One estimate said the procession of the uprooted was 45, 000 refugees long. Most carried only walking sticks. Those able to salvage personal belongings stuffed them into open-sided bullock carts or tied them in sheets and carried them on their heads.

Many didn't make it. At least half a million people were butchered on trains, in cars, or walking on foot. The migration was one of the most murderous outbreaks of sectarian violence in the history of mankind. Scenes of the carnage, visible in old photographs, still shock. Among the now-aged survivors, the scars are still so raw that few want to talk about them.

We arrived some sixty years later, on a warm Sunday afternoon in October of 2007. The Punjab was bucolic. Time had long ago erased physical signs of the carnage. Outbreaks of terrorist violence – suicide bombings by fanatical members of the Taliban, who would like to take over Pakistan, and skirmishes between India and Pakistan in the north, in western Kashmir, seemed far away. We passed easily through broad plains of rich farmland and sheltering trees. Outside one village on the Indian side, a congregation seated on folding chairs under the bright sunshine listened intently to a bearded preacher standing on a platform. Further on, women dressed in bright saris and men wearing turquoise, or red, or yellow turbans vibrant with day glow dye walked slowly along the road or stood in small groups, gossiping. Bullock carts, weathered gray with age and loaded with hay, lumbered along. Small boys herded goats in single file on the road's edge.

Elfie's eyes were bright with excitement. She had grown up in Switzerland and had traveled in much of the world, but she looked with heightened interest at every tree, every animal, every man, every woman. At the border, when the taxi from Amritsar let us out beside an awning-covered restaurant, Elfie looked at me with a warm smile.

"I've crossed many borders but never like this, on foot," she said with delight.

Few foreigners enter Pakistan on foot. Within seconds, a crowd had gathered. Men, women, and children looked at us with intense stares. A skinny little boy ran up to Elfie and handed her a small Indian flag. She smiled and gave him a few coins. He turned and ran into the crowd.

Three porters neatly dressed in blue shirts came up. They lifted our bags onto their heads and led us down a sand-spattered road to a low rectangular building. A few yards away stood the iron border gates, pulled open into ornate brick enclosures.

Before we reached Wagah, I wondered what we would find in Pakistan. I wondered whether I had been wrong in urging Elfie to come. In October of 2007, the government of Pakistan was teetering on the threshold of crisis. Newspapers, magazines, and television broadcasts had been full of warnings that danger lurked everywhere. Assassins had killed political leaders. "Experts" in the United States had called Pakistan a "failed country". They said that it would soon break apart into warring provinces. They warned that anti-Western extremists would grab control, that Pakistan's nuclear weapons would fall into the hands of terrorists, that the streets would run with blood. Magazines ran cover stories with headlines calling Pakistan "The Most Dangerous Place On Earth."

The U.S. Government had long been telling Americans to stay away.

"Due to on-going concerns about the possibility of terrorist activity directed against American citizens and interests," a government

4

Travel Advisory said, "the Department of State continues to warn U.S. Citizens to defer non-essential travel to Pakistan...Al-Quida and Taliban elements continue to operate inside Pakistan, particularly along the porous Afghan border region. Their presence, coupled with that of indigenous sectarian and militant groups in Pakistan, continues to pose potential danger to American citizens."

This was not the Pakistan I knew, a nation that was peaceful, slow-moving, and tranquil. I wondered what had happened. Would we be safe? Would this crisis, intensified by the Taliban and al Qaeda, be worse than other crises I had seen? Where was the country I had come to love headed?

"Pakistan has fascinated me since I was in the Eighth Grade," I told Elfie before we married. "I was at Buckingham Friends School in Pennsylvania. A British diplomat had been visiting the parents of a classmate, and he had come to speak to the entire school, all seventy or so of us."

"England will always be America's ally," he said, "but we have given up our empire and our position of world influence. You, you Americans, now wear the mantle." He paused, looking down at us over half-rim glasses. "Preserving world peace and freedom is on your shoulders."

I liked the idea. It defined a responsibility, a role and a mission for my country, my generation, and maybe myself.

I liked the idea even more when the diplomat showed us slides of some of the countries he said would be our responsibility. One slide showed a picture of two men standing on a wooden bridge over a rocky stream in a green and peaceful valley nestled among snow-covered mountains. Their clothes looked like long-tailed pajamas. Their heads were covered with small woolen caps, tightly rolled. They looked exotic. They looked content. The men, the valley, and the mountains touched something deep inside me.

"This valley is in Hunza, in the northwest part of India," the Englishman said. "It's the Shangri-la of James Hilton's book *Lost*

Horizon. It's the place Kipling wrote about in *The Man Who Would Be King.* It's mentioned in *Kim,* too."

I was then, for a second time, reading Kim, Kipling's picaresque spy novel, and I decided, then and there, that someday I would go to Hunza.

A few years later, when I was home on a break from college, I mentioned it over dinner to a widely-traveled friend of my parents. He had served with U.S. Intelligence in India during the Second World War.

"Hunza's a fascinating place," he said. "Part of Pakistan now. Hard to get to. It's very remote, locked in stupendous mountains. The people are hospitable, self-sufficient, independent. They are supposed to live long lives, very long. You should go there."

A few days later, he sent me a book. It was *Language Hunting in the Karakoram,*[1] written by Elizabeth Lorimer, the wife of Lt. Col. D. L. R. Lorimer, who had been the British political officer in Hunza from 1920 to 1924. When David Lorimer retired a decade later, he and Elizabeth went back. They did not, she wrote, "want to relapse in bath chairs in Cheltenham or Camberly to bewail the old times, the decay of the British Empire and the shortcomings of the young...". They spent fourteen months in Hunza, studying the area's customs and legends and compiling a dictionary of Burushaski, a language spoken only in Hunza, Nagar, Yasin and other remote valleys in the North. Elizabeth Lorimer's descriptions of life in Hunza, the people, the customs, and the tightly knit community ruled by a benevolent hereditary king enticed me more.

Years later, I tried to go to Hunza. It was 1972. The *Reader's Digest,* where I was an associate editor, had assigned me an article which took me to Pakistan. I had a long weekend free. I told a government official that I wanted to visit Hunza.

"That is impossible," he said quickly.

---

1   E.O. Lorimer, Language Hunting in the Karakoram, Karachi, Indus Publications, 1938, 1989, p. 21.

"Why?" I asked. I knew it was far in the north, near the border with China, but...

"It is impossible," he said, again. He paused, seeming to search for a reason. Finally, he said "It is too far."

"Couldn't I fly?"

"Flights are unreliable."

"Could I hire a car and drive?" I asked. I was growing increasingly disappointed.

"There is no road. It is impossible to get there."

He didn't tell me that Hunza, in 1972, was not even formally part of Pakistan. To enter, I would have had to get permission from the Mir, the hereditary ruler, a process that could have taken weeks, if not months. I found that out later, long after I had given up hope of ever going there.

That long-abandoned hope was rekindled years later, in 1986, on a warm Spring afternoon in India. I had been standing beside a road in the foothills of the Himalayas, waiting for a bus, sipping spiced milk tea from a clay cup, and gazing idly at the tattered black road winding its way along the hillside and deep into the forest.

An English traveler I had met on the bus came up beside me.

"Roads fascinate me," I said.

He glanced at the road and said only six words: "I want to travel the KKH."

"The KKH?" I asked.

"It's in Pakistan," he said. "It just opened." His face brightened. The words sped out, and I listened without interrupting. "It's one of the most spectacular roads in the world. It goes from Islamabad up into China. About 900 miles. It passes through the tallest mountains in the world: the Himalayas, the Karakorams, the Hindu Kush. It goes over the Kunjerab Pass, the highest paved road in the world: 16, 500 feet above sea level. Then it goes into Xinjiang, Chinese Turkestan in the old days. It was part of the Silk Road between China and the West."

7

He paused. "The KKH ends at Kashgar, on the western edge of the Taklimakan Desert." He smiled and shook his head. "It means the desert of no return, sort of a Roach Motel of deserts. It's still a relatively unspoiled part of Central Asia."

He paused again, "And, oh, I forgot: the most romantic part. In Pakistan, the KKH goes through Hunza. Have you heard about Hunza?"

"Yes," I said. "I tried to go there once."

"Well, now you can," he said. "On the KKH."

I began planning another trip to Pakistan.

So began a long voyage of discovery. I went to Pakistan four or five more times, often staying for several months each time. Hunza and the Northern Areas became my focal point, but I visited other areas: the commercial metropolis of Karachi, the modern capital of Islamabad, the ancient cities of Lahore, Rawalpindi, and Peshawar, and, in the words of an old song, other "faraway places with strange sounding names."

I had fallen in love with the country and the people.

Now, I was returning with Elfie.

Wagah is midway between Lahore in Pakistan and Amritsar in India. The Indian immigration checkpoint at Wagah was a one story building, set in a field a ten minute walk from the restaurant where the taxi had left us and a few yards from the brick enclosed border crossing. The porters led us inside. They eased our luggage onto drab, gray marble floors, and slid down beside it, resting their backs against the gray walls. Two Indian immigration officials sat at low counters behind thick Plexiglas. We were the only people in the cavernous lobby except for a young traveler, who was having trouble explaining something about his passport.

"No," he said. "I was born in Berlin." He put his index finger on an open page of the passport. "Berlin. Berlin. The capital of Germany. Berlin. I am German."

The officials looked at him blankly.

He turned to Elfie. "How can it take so long?" he asked in German. He turned back to the counter. One of the officials looked again at his passport and loudly stamped it. The German turned and left, a disgusted look on his face.

The officials took our passports. They looked at the photographs and then at us. They looked at the page with our visas and stamped our passports without a word.

We were free to leave India.

Three new porters, Pakistanis, picked up our luggage. They led us along a long, narrow road and onto the edge of a sun-baked field. Three Pakistani Border Rangers, dressed in crisply starched khaki uniforms, their legs stretched out, sat casually on plastic chairs at small, khaki draped card tables in the shade of a lone tree. It was the Pakistan checkpoint.

One of the Rangers took our passports. He looked perfunctorily at our visas. He stamped the passports and handed them back to us.

"Welcome to Pakistan," he said with a smile.

The warmth of the welcome made me feel like I was returning home. Elfie's eyes were wide with curiosity.

The porters led us to a sparkling new customs building a few yards away. Except for a few Pakistani men, the room was empty. The porters put our luggage on the floor beside a large X-ray machine. A man wearing a Pakistani customs badge came over. He looked at the bags.

"Do you have any alcohol?" he asked. I had been asked that question every time I had entered Pakistan. I was prepared.

"One bottle of Scotch whiskey," I said. "Laphroaig. It's for medicinal purposes. I have a doctor's prescription."

He waved me on.

Saeed Anwar Khan had e-mailed me that two of his nephews would meet us. I looked around. No one was looking for us.

An official in a blue suit came out of a small office. "Are you the two Americans?" he asked.

I wasn't sure whether to answer him. I thought of the State Department warning.

"Mr. Shuman?" he asked.

I nodded yes.

"Follow me," he said. He led us back onto the road. The porters followed, our baggage on their heads.

Elfie noticed that her Indian flag had disappeared.

"Have you seen my little flag?" she asked one of the porters.

"Madam," he said emphatically, "you are now in Pakistan."

We came to a tree-shaded sidewalk alongside a two-story building. On our left was a garden with white metal tables and chairs and a man, a woman, and two children drinking tea. Ahead of us, across a concrete driveway, was a long gray building. A small sign read "PTDC, Pakistan Tourist Development Corporation Motel."

The inside was dark and worn. It smelled of curries and tobacco smoke. One end of the long room was set with tables and chairs. A buffet table topped with battered copper warming pans rested against the wall. A man and woman and three small children were seated at a table. A tall, long-bearded man in a brown sleeveless sweater pulled over a shalwar kameez, the long-tailed national dress of Pakistan, was serving them plates heaped high with boiled white rice and chicken drenched in a heavy brown sauce, so pungent we could smell it half a room away.

We sat on low couches facing the manager's office. The walls were hung with travel posters showing the wonders of Pakistan: mountains, deserts, red sandstone forts, Lahore's Shalimar Gardens, and the ruins of an abandoned and ancient city, Mohenjodaro, one of the greatest cities of the long-lost Indus Valley Civilization.

Elfie looked carefully at the pictures. "This is so exciting," she said.

I was pleased. "You'll love it," I said.

A few minutes later, two men, immaculately dressed in casual Western clothes, walked over.

"Welcome to Pakistan," the older one, who I judged to be in his early forties, said. "I am Arshad Ali. I am Saeed's nephew. We have been waiting for you since yesterday." He turned to the younger man, who had a mischievous glint in his eyes. "This is Shabir Ahmed, my cousin. He's also Saeed's nephew."

We shook hands. "Would you like some lunch?" Arshad asked.

"No, thank you," I said. We had eaten a snack on the plane from New Delhi.

They left to finish their own lunch.

The bearded waiter brought us tea.

The hotel manager, young and gracious, sat on a chair facing us.

"I hope you have a good trip," he said. "You have come at an interesting time. No one knows what's going to happen."

"Yes," I agreed. "The Musharraf government seems about to fall. But isn't there a broader issue? I don't want to be too intellectual, but it seems to me that Pakistan is a battlefield between two ideas of how people should be governed. One is the Taliban way, which is medieval and authoritarian. The other is the modern way, which is innovative and free. As an outside observer, it seems to me to be a fight over what kind of a nation Pakistan should be."

"Yes," he said. "An interesting time."

Arshad and Shabir returned.

"We'll load the luggage," Arshad said. He picked up Elfie's black canvas case and took it to a gray Toyota SUV parked beside the hotel.

"Would you like to see the flag lowering ceremony?" Arshad asked. "The closing of the border gates?"

He led us to concrete benches at the edge of the road. Shabir followed. I wondered if he was providing security like the Secret Service agents I knew when I served as an assistant to President Ford. He was just being polite. We sat on the benches. The border gates were a few feet away. Behind us, rows of crowded concrete bleachers overlooked the roadway and the Indian side of the border. One side was filled with men. Most were wearing short sleeved shirts and trousers. The other side was filled with women wearing brightly colored head scarves. A band played. A stocky man wearing a bright green T-shirt with the star and crescent symbol of Pakistan on the front walked onto the road. He jumped up and down and waved his hands like an orchestra conductor. He was a cheerleader.

The crowd quickly responded.

"Pakistan Zindabad [Long Live Pakistan] they shouted.

Across the border, the answer came back from crowded bleachers.

"Jai Hind" [Long live India].

"Pakistan Zindabad,"

"Jai Hind."

The ceremony began.

Two Pakistani Rangers marched past us. Their faces were frozen in mock anger. They were wearing black shalwar kameez with blood red sashes. Raven black plumes rested on their heads. They goose stepped in long, loud strides toward the open gate. At the border line, two Indian officers, dressed in freshly pressed khaki, were waiting. The Pakistanis stopped a few feet away, loudly stamping their heavy-soled boots on the black tarmac. More Pakistani Rangers, sporting bristling mustaches, goose stepped to the crossing line and joined them, exchanging fierce glances with the Indians.

Two officers, one Indian, one Pakistani, approached each other. Stiffly, they shook hands across the white border line. They stepped back and stood rigidly at attention as other soldiers lowered, slowly and in unison, the Pakistani and Indian flags, which had been flying from high poles planted at each side of the gates.

The people in the stands were still. Only the clamping of boots and the snorts of the Rangers broke the silence. Soldiers on each side folded the flags precisely. They executed an abrupt military about-face and carried the flags away, holding them in outstretched arms like offerings to a king. The Pakistani and Indian officers returned to the white borderline. Again, formally and with grim faces, they shook hands. They stepped back. The gates rolled shut, meeting with a loud clang.

The hostilities between India and Pakistan, which had led to three major wars, the loss of the eastern part of Pakistan, which became Bangladesh in 1972, constant skirmishes over the state of Kashmir, and Pakistan's endemic fears of an attack by India, were reduced to comic opera.

At least for now.

At this border.

2

"How far is Lahore?" Elfie asked when we reached the car.

"Not far," Arshad said. "About eighteen miles."

The road was congested. Shabir took a short cut. The SUV swayed as we drove over a rutted dirt road alongside an open field. Bushes brushed against the side of the car. Low tree limbs swept the roof. It took us about five minutes to reach the paved road, a four-lane highway. A sluggish irrigation canal divided it. Trees shaded it from Pakistan's almost constant sun. Its narrow lanes were packed with every form of human transportation: pedestrians, bicycles, motorcycles, cars, vans, buses, brightly decorated trucks, bullock carts, horse-drawn rickshaws. Alongside the road, in depressions lined with the litter of wind-blown white plastic bags, boys played cricket.

We stopped for a traffic light. An overloaded white van pulled up next to us. Men and women were squeezed together on narrow seats and they stared at us, never blinking. Two young men approached our car. They touched the windows with aluminum trays of sectioned coconuts.

"Do you want a piece of coconut?" I asked Elfie.

She looked skeptically at the trays. "I think I'll wait," she said.

We reached an intersection. Shabir made a sharp right turn.

"This is the Grand Trunk Road," Arshad said.

The GTR as it is known in acronym-happy Pakistan, is one of the oldest roads in the world. It was built to link Kabul in Afghanistan with the eastern part of India. Rudyard Kipling described it in *Kim* as "a river of life as nowhere else exists in the world." Even today, it was packed with every form of life: people, chickens, goats, bullocks. High above the roadway, two huge billboards stood in colorful contrast. One advertised VISA credit cards. One advertised Nokia cell phones.

"Those signs say a lot about Pakistan," I told Elfie. "This road is chaotic. Too many people, too much traffic. I don't think it has changed much since Kipling's day. But the signs tell of another Pakistan, a modern world of international banking and instant international communication. That's one of the things that fascinates me. Pakistan is a nation of contrasts, ancient and modern, with great wealth and grim poverty."

Elfie nodded. I could tell she was excited in anticipation of what was to come.

As we neared Lahore, traffic diminished. We passed large houses set back from the road, some behind high walls, others on verdant, well-manicured lawns. It looked like an expensive English suburb. I thought of a car I had fallen in love with on my first trip to Pakistan. It was a silver Rolls Royce convertible sedan, top down, made in the 1930's and parked in a driveway. I had wanted to buy it. Except I didn't have the money and it probably wasn't for sale.

"Lahore was the first city I saw in Pakistan, and I was fascinated," I said as we entered Lahore itself and traffic again became congested. "Lahore was once considered one of the world's most beautiful cities. In Mogul times, it was the capitol of India. The Moguls built gems of architecture. Once, I spent several days just looking at buildings: The giant red sandstone fort, the white-domed mosque next to it, and innumerable tombs, peaceful in their architectural symmetry and glazed tile facades. And, outside the city itself, I spent several hours at the Shalimar gardens. They brightened up a dusty, hot afternoon. Emperor Shah Jehan built them as a formal oasis of water and trees in the arid desert. To irrigate it, he built canals to bring water from Kashmir, more than 100 miles away."

I smiled in remembrance. "Shah Jehan was the emperor who drove his kingdom to bankruptcy building the Taj Mahal, south of Delhi," I added.

Lahore is no longer one of the world's most beautiful cities. Time, an explosion of people, and neglect have aged Lahore unkindly. We passed a line of stores, banks, modern office buildings with plate glass windows, hotels, restaurants, even a YMCA, all pressed against the sidewalks. Still, it was exotic, with touches of history everywhere.

An unpretentious rectangular wooden building with a shaded porch caught my attention.

"That looks British," I said.

"Like something in a picture book," Elfie said.

"Yes," I replied. "And a lot less grand than most of the British buildings. Most were built in a style called Mogul Gothic. It combined Islamic architecture with something that looked like stolid Victorian railway stations. But they have a certain charm. I particularly like the National Museum. Its first curator, incidentally, was Rudyard Kipling's father, John Lockwood Kipling."

"Remember the cannon from Kim?" I continued. "At the beginning of the novel where Kim is playing, as Kipling said, 'in defiance of municipal orders'. It's across from the Lahore Museum which, to quote Kipling again, was 'Ajaib-Gher – the Wonder House as the natives call the Lahore Museum.'"

She smiled.

"I like Kim's cannon," I said. "It was called Zam-zamah, and once it was the last word in weaponry. It had a sister cannon, but that fell off a barge and was lost in the Chenab River. They were the largest cannons made in Asia. For nearly 100 years Kim's cannon was a most fearful weapon. It was taken out of service only after it cracked at the battle of Multan. Then, it could never be used again, except as a symbol of military power. The British, always conscious of symbols, planted it in the middle of the Mall, the main thoroughfare. As Kipling wrote," Zam-zamah was so powerful a symbol that, 'Who hold Zam-zamah, that fire breathing dragon, hold the Punjab, for the great green-bronze piece is always first of the conqueror's loot.'"

"You've memorized that?" Elfie asked.

"Yes," I answered. "Totally useless information, but I always loved the imagery of the ragged boy Kim playing on the cannon. It's a good start for an exciting spy story."

I looked out at the familiar streets as Shabir wove our way through the heavy traffic on the Mall.

"We should be passing the museum in a minute or so," I said, "and there will be Kim's cannon."

We would be disappointed. Shabir turned off the Mall. Suddenly, we were in a congested area of narrow streets and three story buildings.

"What is this?" I asked Arshad.

"Anarkali," he said, "the old city. It is supposed to be one of the oldest markets in South Asia. It was named after Emperor Akbar's favorite concubine, some four hundred years ago. She had a love affair with his son and he had her killed, buried alive. The son, when he became Emperor Jahangir, built a tomb for her. It was a predecessor to the Taj Mahal."

The streets were pitted with potholes. Shoppers walked briskly by, expressionless, absorbed in errands. Clothing and pottery and other goods for sale were displayed on the sidewalks. A block away, a dark blue awning extended out to the street. White lettering on the sides spelled out "Mirage Hotel." Shabir drove the car into a parking place on the sidewalk. A bearded security guard in a dark blue uniform and a dark blue beret watched us intently. His hands rested on a battered rifle slung over his shoulder. We went in and registered.

I had told Saeed that I wanted to stay in a modest hotel. The manager of the Mirage showed us three rooms. All were sparsely furnished. The Mirage was a far cry from the elegant Oberoi Hotel in New Delhi, where we had stayed the previous four nights. We had gone first to India to spend an evening with Kushwant Singh, one of India's greatest writers and author of *Train to Pakistan,* the classic novel about the bloodshed after the partition of India and Pakistan.

At the Mirage, we chose the room with a Western toilet, but Elfie grimaced.

"Can we get some toilet paper?" she asked. She had yet to discover that in many places toilet paper is a luxury. The manager left. He returned a few minutes later with a roll of toilet paper and a table, two chairs, and towels.

3

The next day, we drove to a new section of Lahore. We had an appointment with Arif Zaman, a professor of mathematics and statistics at the Lahore University of Management Sciences, one of Pakistan's best universities. Shabir parked in the courtyard of a spacious house behind gated walls on a quiet street. Children's book bags and a pair of shoes were scattered on the steps. Arif greeted us at the door. He is in his late forties. His beard and hair, which he wears long, are gray. He was wearing light gray shalwar kameez and a gray cap.

"Welcome," he said with a broad smile. He seemed very American, a college professor who had retained many of the youthful open and informal qualities of an undergraduate.

Zaman had studied at Harvey Mudd College, a part of the Claremont group near Los Angeles. He had rented a room from Edith Cole, a school psychologist, and had fallen in love with her daughter, Sarah. They had married, and he went on to earn a PhD from Stanford University and to teach mathematics and statistics at Purdue and Florida State before returning to Pakistan, where he had grown up.

I later learned that he was a member of Tablighi Jamaat, a group set up in the late 1920s "to deliver the message of Islam." It is a revivalist organization that eschews politics and violence in its quest to reform society.

We were entering a deeply observant household.

Arif showed Elfie through a door to the right of the entry. I could hear children laughing but I was not invited inside. It was the women's section of the house. Elfie went in carrying small presents for Sarah and the children.

Arif led Arshad, Shabir and me into a room on the left. It was his bedroom. It was furnished with a large double bed, bookshelves and a large leather electric massage chair.

I sat in the massage chair. Arif turned it on, and the rollers kneaded my back muscles, still stiff from days of travelling. Arshad and Shabir sat in wooden chairs next to a bookcase. Arif sat on the bed, with his bare feet under him.

"Pakistan is more interesting than the United States," Arif said. "Pakistan has different regions. Each is unique, different topographically, historically, culturally, and in their interpretation of Islam. In the United States, every place looks the same. Once, in Florida, I was driving from Tallahassee with friends and when I woke up after a nap, I didn't know where we were. The roads and cities all looked alike."

We had gone to see him to talk about the school for Afghan Refugee girls outside of Peshawar. The advisory committee to which we belong is largely made up of Quakers in Southern California. Arif was one of the people who had suggested that the school be established after the attacks on the United States on September 11, 2001.

His mother-in-law, Edith Cole, a Quaker, had told us that "I wanted to show that Americans can do more than drop bombs." And being a Quaker, a sect that does not try to convert people, she didn't want to proselytize. "We left the Bible out of it," she said.

"How is the school doing?" I asked Arif.

"The school is doing well," he said. "But I am not sure it should be continued. The situation has changed in Afghanistan. Many Afghanis are returning home."

"We'll raise the question when we go to the school," I said.

4

Arshad suggested we have dinner at the Village Restaurant.

The driveway was jammed with BMWs, Mercedes, and Land Rovers. Shabir let us out at the front door.

The restaurant was housed in a reproduction of a large, mud-walled, village house. A costumed doorman, wearing a tall Punjabi plume, held the door open. The walls of the lobby were hung with photographs of famous guests. One was President Musharraf in an open-necked shirt. Next to it was a photograph of Princess Diana of Wales. She was standing where we were standing, smiling happily. She seemed at home in this artificially rustic building so far from the splendor of Buckingham Palace.

"She had been in love with a Pakistani doctor," Elfie told me, "but she was rejected by his family."

"How do you know that?" I asked.

"I read it in one of the biographies written about her," she replied.

Arshad got us a table. Shabir joined us. We walked through the buffet section.

For most Americans, a knowledge of South Asian food, Pakistani or Indian, derives from mid-priced restaurants which seem to cook one pot of heavily curried sauce and spoon it over everything: chicken, lamb, even fish. Good South Asian food is more subtle, a harmonious blend of spices and herbs. Some is grilled. Some is roasted. Some is baked. The "curries" are complex and flavorful sauces.

At the Village Restaurant, the food was freshly cooked and varied. Cooks in white aprons and high white hats stood beside the red coals of low fires or beside large flat pans along the walls. Frying fish crackled in hot oil. Sheekh kabab on shiny steel rods dripped juices onto hot coals. Nearby, copper pots filled with rice, dal, or spinach rested on cloth-covered tables. Small wheeled carts, such as might be used by street food vendors, sat in the center of the room. In another section, a roasted lamb was warming in a glass walled cabinet. Costumed servers, all men, dispensed ice cream, cotton candy, and traditional Pakistani sweets to small children, some dressed in jeans, some in embroidered shalwar kameez. One boy, about ten years old, wore white leggings with tiny silver bells sewn on the legs. The bells jingled as he walked. Another boy, about the same age, wore a white suit and a necktie. The bottom hem of his jacket was brightly embroidered.

Customers strolled around, picking food from platters heaped high on the tables. The men were dressed in Western suits, jeans, or dark trousers and open shirts. Most of the women were dressed in bright colors. Most wore head scarves. Eight women, sitting at a long table, wore black burkas that enveloped their heads and left only a small strip of skin exposed for their eyes.

"Taliban," Shabir said in a low voice.

"I wonder how they eat with their mouths covered," I whispered to Elfie.

She didn't answer. She only shrugged her shoulders.

"This is supposed to look like the common areas of a traditional village," Arshad explained as he walked us to our table.

A waiter came to the table. We ordered Coca-Cola and went back to the common area to pick out our food. Elfie looked over all the food on display. She chose cooked vegetables, rice, and lots of mangoes. I had a cook slice off a piece of the lamb and served myself rice and spinach from copper kettles on a nearby table.

We returned to our table. Three musicians, a flutist, a drummer, and a harmonium player, began playing a few feet away.

"What is the music?" I asked.

"Folk tunes," Arshad said.

Folk music is often the key to a civilization. It reflects the traditions, legends and culture of a people.

"Did any of the music come from the Indus Valley Civilization?" I asked Arshad.

"It's old, but no one knows," he said.

"I wonder if the IVC left any traces, besides the ruins that have been discovered," I added. "I know that a satellite photograph of the Indus Valley would show all of modern-day Pakistan, But did the IVC influence Pakistan's modern government, social behavior, customs?"

"We can ask tomorrow when we go to the department of archeology," he said.

5

The Indus Valley Civilization was, emerging evidence suggests, the greatest of the world's ancient civilizations. It was the largest known civilization of the Bronze Age, larger than Egypt, Sumer, China, or anything in Meso-America. Yet it lay forgotten for nearly 5, 000 years, not discovered until the Nineteenth Century, and then only by chance.

The chance came in the form of a deserter from the army of the British East India Company. His name was James Lewis. His story offers a glimpse of India and Pakistan in the days of the British Raj, and of British efforts to learn the history of the Subcontinent.

Lewis was the son of a prosperous London merchant. He had been educated at a small independent school in Walthamstow, northeast of London. He was fluent in French, knew Latin and Greek, and was fascinated by Alexander the Great, especially Alexander's campaign in Afghanistan and India. In 1821, he was working as a clerk at Durant & Co., London silk and insurance brokers. He was twenty-one, and he was bored.

One day, he had a quarrel with his father. He enlisted as an infantryman in the British East India Company's Bengal Artillery. He fought during the Jat Wars at the second siege of Bharatpur in January 1826, during which 14, 000 troops were wounded or killed, but most of the time he was assigned to the staff of the Commandant, Maj. Gen. Hardwick, arranging and depicting zoological specimens for publication. It was not the adventure he had been looking for.

On July 4, 1827, he decided to desert. His regiment was stationed at Agra, and he and another soldier, Richard Potter, slipped out of camp. They walked west, across the treacherous Thar Desert, heading for Afghanistan. They hoped to support themselves as military advisers to a local ruler.

Crossing the Indian desert in the height of summer was arduous, and they had little money. Within weeks, they had worn out their shoes, their clothes were filthy, Lewis' red hair was dirty and tangled, and they were frequently sick. Finding work began to seem impossible, for they were outlaws. Desertion was a high crime. The East India Company had posted notices in every British garrison in the subcontinent, seeking their return.

They tried to change their identity. Lewis called himself Charles Masson and said he was from Kentucky. Porter, unimaginatively, changed his name to John Brown. Still, no local prince would hire them.

At Ahmadpur, south of Multan, in what is now Pakistan, their luck changed. They met a Pennsylvania-born Quaker. His name was Josiah Harlan. He was organizing a small army to march into Afghanistan and take advantage of fratricidal frictions in the ruling family to make himself king. His story was the inspiration for Kipling's famous novella, *The Man Who Would Be King.*

Harlan recognized Masson and Brown as deserters, but he felt they could be useful. They had carefully kept their British uniforms and broadswords and they spoke English. Harlan made them his mounted orderlies. They rode together as friends, leading their small army across the Indus and into Afghanistan.

But Masson deserted again.

Alone, he went back toward India, trying to follow Alexander's route. He had, as his biographer wrote, "already studied with some thoroughness the routes of Alexander the Great on his Persian and Indian campaigns...".

In 1828, outside Harappa, in the center of what is now Pakistan, Masson camped among the scattered ruins of a large city. He knew it was ancient. He assumed it was Buddhist, for Buddhists had built scores of cities in the western part of India. As he later noted in his book *Narrative of Various Journeys in Balochistan, Afghanistan and The Panjab*, "Tradition affirms the existence here of a city, so considerable that it extended to Chicha Watni, thirteen cosses distant...' [13 to 39 miles; a coss is about one to three miles].

He collected a few coins, a few seals, and other small artifacts. Then, he went back to explore Afghanistan. Eventually, he produced the first comprehensive archaeological records of eastern Afghanistan. He became so noted as an archaeologist and numismatist that the British pardoned him for deserting and enlisted him as a "newswriter," the cover word for spy.

No one realized the importance of his discoveries at Harappa. The area lay unexplored for nearly a quarter of a century.

In the 1850's, British engineers built a railroad from Lahore to Multan, some two hundred miles to the south. For ballast, they crushed the dried brick walls of the buildings at Harappa, destroying the upper levels of the city and, with it, irreplaceable evidence of one of mankind's earliest civilizations.

In the mid-1800s, Sir Alexander Cunningham, director of the recently formed Archaeological Survey of India, led an expedition to Harappa. Early Chinese pilgrims had written of ancient Buddhist cities and he hoped to find the remnants of what they had described. He found what Masson had found: a few bits of ancient pottery, a few stone tools, some worked shell, and a badly worn soapstone seal. The seal had a knob on the back with a small hole. On the front was a strange one-horned animal resembling a bull with no hump. Above the animal was a short inscription in a script that did not relate to any known writing. He went away disappointed, but he sought no explanation of what he had found.

Some seventy years later, in 1920, John Marshall, director of the Archeology Survey, sent a field officer, Daya Ram Sahai, to Harappa to begin new excavations. A year later, he sent another archaeologist, Rakhal Das Banerji, to Mohenjodaro, in Sindh, three hundred and forty miles to the south. Marshall believed that both sites were Buddhist.

At Moehenjodaro, Banerji discovered a ruined Buddhist stupa. More important, he found the remains of a well-planned city. It had massive brick buildings, streets laid out in a grid, and elaborate sewage systems. He found seals and ceramics, stone sculptures, bronze tools, gold ornaments and cubical chert weights similar to those found at Harappa.

Marshall realized the importance of Banerji's findings. He announced the discovery of a civilization, older than any previously known in the Indian subcontinent. He did not estimate how old it was. He only suggested that it had lasted for several centuries and had disappeared before the rise of the Mauryan Empire in the Third Century BC. He said it had not come from regions to the west; it had developed in the Indus Valley itself. He published his findings with photographs of the seals and tablets and other objects in *The Illustrated London News* of September 20th 1924. Within a week, scholars who had discovered similar seals at ancient Susa in southwestern Iran dating to the mid-Third Century millennium BC, wrote him reporting their own findings or asking for more information.

I first heard of the Indus Valley Civilization in 1988 in Washington, DC. The press attache' of the Pakistan Embassy, Malik Zahor Ahmed, had introduced me to Dr. Jonathan Mark Kenoyer, professor of archeology at the University of Wisconsin.

Kenoyer is one of the world's leading authorities on the Indus Valley Civilization.

We met for coffee at a Connecticut Avenue bookstore. Kenoyer was tall, blond, and he wore a gold ring in one ear.

"The Indus civilization," he told me, "may have had more than 2, 000 city states. They were scattered along the Indus River and its tributaries, from what is now Afghanistan eastward into present day India. They extended from the Arabian Sea northward to the mountains that now form Pakistan's border with China. They covered about 400, 000 square miles, an area considerably larger than all the states on the East Coast of the United States, from Maine to Florida, bigger than the British Isles. They were an agricultural and trading civilization, reaching to all the known world. Moenjodaro in the south, and Harappa, in the center of Pakistan, were its two greatest cities. And, the Indus civilization was unique."

"In what way?" I asked.

"They were not warlike," he said. "We've found only a small amount of evidence of warfare or captive taking."

In the years since 1924, nearly 1,000 archaeologists have tried to solve the mysteries of the Indus civilization. Scholarly explanations differ widely. Some archaeologists believe that the people of the Indus Valley had no written language. Others, trying to interpret the writing on the more than 2, 000 seals and tablets in museums, believe that the long-lost language was a precursor of modern Sanskrit. Others believe it was Dravidian, a language similar to Sanskrit and now spoken mainly in South India.

No one has found a key to the mystery. Until, maybe, now.

A few years ago, three researchers offered an answer. They are Asko Parpola of the University of Helsinki, who has written much on the Indus Script, Kurt Schildmann, a linguist at the German Ministry of Defense, and Rainer Hasenpflug, a German student of the Indus Civilization.

In their book *Inscriptions of the Indus Civilization,* published in 2006, they theorized that the language was an ancient version of Sanskrit and that it was an Indo-European language related to Greek and Latin. They translated the more than 2, 000 seals and tablets in museums. The translations revealed a highly sophisticated culture. It was multi-racial and multi-cultural. It had sages, priests, philosophers, scientists, mathematicians, musicians, farmers, merchants, and a warrior caste. It traded with other great civilizations in Arabia, Africa, and the Middle East. It was a precursor in its languages, myths, religion, social and cultural life, crafts and traditions to the culture and identity of modern India.

Most likely, it – the Indus Valley Civilization – not Egypt or Sumer, was the cradle of civilization.

Arshad, who had studied to be an archaeologist, took Elfie and me to see Shahbaz Khan, director of Punjab's Department of Archeology. He is balding, slender, and soft spoken. We were joined by Afzal Khan, Director of the Lahore Fort and formerly director of archaeological research at Mohenjodaro.

"Little archaeological work is being done, now," Dr. Shahbaz told us. "We once had one person from the Archeology Department working with foreign archaeologists, American, French, British, and even some Japanese and Koreans, who were mainly interested in a later civilization, the Buddhists. But now, with the political situation, it is too dangerous for archaeologists. There is much we need to discover."

"Why do you think the Indus Civilization disappeared?" Elfie asked.

Afzal Khan answered. "We believe that there may have been several reasons," he said. "It used to be believed that the Saraswati River dried up and that that forced people into more agriculturally productive regions. That is no longer true. It is also not true that there was an invasion of Aryans from the north. We could find no evidence of attacks, of looting, or fires. The Aryan migration to the

Indus Valley seems to have been a peaceful one. Now, we believe that the causes were over-population and deforestation because of lack of rain. People migrated to other areas, mainly along the Ganges in India, looking for new fields."

"So," I said, "the Indus Civilization did not decline and fall. It just moved east. But did it have any effect on present-day Pakistan? Did it leave any cultural beliefs or practices?"

"No," Afzal Khan said. "We know they were traders, and peaceful, and that they left artifacts, seals, tablets, jewelry. They did not bury valuable ornaments or gold with the dead. The jewelry and gold continued in circulation." Some are still in use."

He leaned back in his chair.

"Once, at Moehenjodaro," he continued, "I noticed that the seals the laundryman had used to identify my clothes were identical to seals found on clay tablets in the ruins. I asked, where did this seal design come from?"

"I learned it from my grandfather," the laundryman said. "He told me he had learned it from his grandfather."

"But they left no political or social system?" I asked.

"No," he said.

The culture which most influenced modern Pakistan, I realized, was Islam, mixed with British and earlier influences.

6

I wanted to find out more about the formation of Pakistan. Why was India split apart, "vivisected" in the words of Mohandus Gandhi, to create two separate nations? Why couldn't India's Muslims work in the framework of the secular society India was hoping to be? What were the dreams of Pakistan's founders? Was Pakistan to be secular Muslim nation or rigidly religious? Was it to be tolerant or intolerant of other religions? Was it to be adaptable to changing ways, to practice Ijtihad, a process laid out in the Koran to continually rethink and modify Islamic practices? Or was it to be based on a strict, intolerant and unchanging interpretation of Islam that has given rise to the Taliban and attacks against the West, ritual beheadings, and the banning of such "un-Islamic" activities as selling DVDs, watching cable television, singing and dancing, shaving beards, allowing girls to attend school, or even criticizing the Taliban?

7

We went to see Javid Iqbal, the son of Allama Muhammad Iqbal, one of Pakistan's founders.

Walking up the long driveway to his Western-style house in Lahore, we passed three white marble lawn statues near the front door. One statue was of a man dancing, his long robe swinging from his body. Another was sitting on the lawn playing a drum. The other, also sitting, was playing a long horn.

"Sufis?" Elfie asked.

"Yes," I replied. "Dervishes."

Sufis are a mystical sect in Islam. Three hundred years ago, they were a major force in converting the people of western India from Buddhism and local tribal religions to Islam. Islam had come from Arabia with sailors and merchants and armies beginning about the Eighth Century, AD, about one hundred years after the death of the Prophet Mohamed. The Sufis did most of the actual conversions. They preached a religion of equality, unity, and the worship of one god. Gradually, Muslims controlled a large portion of the Indian subcontinent. The great buildings associated with India, the forts, the palaces, and the ornate tombs, such as the Taj Mahal, were built under Mogul emperors. But by the mid-1700's Mogul power weakened, and the British moved in.

Their major instrument was the British East India Company, chartered by Queen Elizabeth I on December 31, 1600, as a merchant trading company. It expanded. By the mid-1700's, it began to take over the functions of government. The British drew political borders, built highways and railroads and irrigation canals, provided disaster relief, levied taxes, and administered laws. They also placed ambitious Hindus in administrative positions, further whittling away Muslim power.

In 1857, a small group of Indians tried to throw the British out. The Indians called it the first fight for independence. The British called it the Sepoy Rebellion and ruthlessly put it down, adopting such Mogul tactics as putting prisoners in front of cannon barrels and then firing the cannon.

The reaction of the British Government in London was to take control of the East India Company and other smaller chartered ventures. In 1877, Queen Victoria assumed the title *Empress of India*. India became the crown jewel in the British Empire.

The Indians still wanted independence. By the start of the Twentieth Century, an independence movement was strong and well organized.

"It will be interesting to talk with Javid Iqbal," I said as we approached the front door.. "His father was one of the leaders of the independence movement."

Initially, India's Muslims did not seek a state separate from the rest of India. They wanted only to block attempts by Hindu society to absorb them. Islam and Hinduism, they believed, were two social systems that had given rise to two different cultures. They could not co-exist. Gandhi thought the issue could be resolved by having Hindu and Muslim communities hold separate elections. The Muslims, after years of discussions, split with Gandhi. Javid Iqbal's father, Muhammad Iqbal, felt that an independent India, with Muslims as only one part of a secular electorate would further weaken the foundations of Islam and Muslim society, and that India's Hindu majority would crowd out Muslim heritage, culture, and political influence.

In 1930, in a speech, to a meeting of the All India Muslim League, in Allahabad, Muhammad Iqbal proposed the creation of what he called "an amalgamated state" as a national homeland for, at least, the Muslims of North West India. Mohammad Iqbal was President of the Muslim League. He was an impressive man. He was an astute lawyer, trained at the Inn of Lincoln's Court in London. He had returned to India to help throw out the British. He also was a distinguished poet in a culture where poetry is a high form of art, both temporal and spiritual. He was the leading Muslim philosopher in South Asia. He is buried in a modest tomb right next to the red sandstone fort in Lahore. His tomb is pictured on the two rupee note.

"Iqbal believed that Islam needed to be revitalized, that it had declined over the centuries," I continued. "He felt the world was becoming too materialistic, that it was loosing its spirituality. He hoped Islam could bring it back. His proposal for a separate Muslim nation in the Indian subcontinent was a radical and controversial idea. It became even more controversial when a group of Muslim students at Cambridge University, led by a student named Rahmat Ali, gave it a name: Pakistan."

We stopped to look at the Sufi statues.

"The students had formed an organization," I said. "They called it the Pakistan National Movement and explained the name in a pamphlet published in 1933. "The name Pakistan," they said, was "composed of letters taken from our homelands: that is Punjab, Afghana (the North West Frontier Province), Kashmir, Iran, Sind, Tukharistan, Afghanistan, and Baluchistan. It means land of the Paks, the spiritually pure and clean."

"Ah," Elfie said, "It's interesting how countries get their names. I've often wondered."

"That's the story behind the name," I said. "But not everyone liked the name Pakistan. In the early 1930's, the Muslim leaders, including Iqbal, were not ready to talk of an independent Muslim state in northwest India. It did not fit their political strategy. Iqbal would have nothing to do with the Rahmat Ali plan. Another British-trained lawyer, Muhammad Ali Jinnah, who was Pakistan's first head of state and who would later be known as Quaid-i-Islam, or the Great Leader, also opposed it.

Frank Moraes, a distinguished Indian editor and writer, wrote in his book *Witness to an Era: India 1920 to Present Day*,[2] "I noticed a distinct lift of Jinnah's eyebrows whenever I happened to mention Rahmat Ali. He seemed to regard Rahmat Ali's concept of Pakistan as some sort of Walt Disney dreamland, if not Wellsian nightmare, and I think he felt the professional's contempt for the amateur's mistake of showing his hand without holding the trumps."

2   Quoted in Javid Iqbal, Islam and Pakistan's Identity, Lahore, Sang-e-Meel Publications, 2007, p273-4.

8

We reached the front door. I pushed the bell.

Javid Iqbal opened the door. He was in his mid-eighties but looked much younger, with receding hair turning to gray. He was wearing a white shalwar kameez. A blue ascot was tied around his neck. In the pocket of his long gray vest were two ballpoint pens, one red, the other blue.

"Dr. Iqbal?" I asked, and introduced myself and Elfie.

Javid Iqbal is one of Pakistan's most distinguished citizens. He earned a PhD at Cambridge University and became a Barrister-at-Law at Lincoln's Court, London. He has served as a Judge of the Supreme Court of Pakistan, as Chief Justice of the Lahore High Court, as a roving ambassador for Pakistan, and as an elected member of the Senate of Pakistan. He twice served as Pakistan's delegate to the United Nations General Assembly. He has received honorary degrees from Villanova University outside Philadelphia and Selcuk University in Konya, Turkey.

He is a prolific and insightful writer. He has written books and papers on Islamic political thought, political ideology in Pakistan and the philosophy and works of Muhammad Iqbal, his father.

He led us to the living room.

A servant brought tea and cookies.

"What was the founding dream of Pakistan?" I asked.

"Pakistan was to be a new experiment," Justice Iqbal said. "It was a novel solution to a political problem. There had always been a clash of cultures in India. Only the Emperor Ashoka, two hundred years before the birth of Christ, had held it together. The first book on the clash of civilizations was written in 1000 AD. It seems contemporary today.

"The distance between ideology and reality is the main cause behind Pakistan's quest for identity," he continued. "The crucial question for modern Muslims in Pakistan is: What is an Islamic state? Has it ever been established or is it only an aspiration? Muhammad Iqbal believed, as the Prophet Mohammad originally taught, that the ideal government was a cooperative venture between the leaders and the people. It was a republican ideal, with continual discussions between the people and their leaders. Islam, he believed, provided the guidelines of how best our earthly lives can be lived down here below."

"Is Islam rigid?" I asked. "Did your father and the other founders allow for changes in world conditions, for new technology, for example? Or did they think the laws and practices laid down in the Seventh Century should never be changed?"

"Muhammad Iqbal," he said, "believed, as I do, in a reconstructive interpretation of Islam."

I looked puzzled.

"Reconstructive," he explained, "is an interpretation that seeks to blend tradition with modernity in an effort to reform society. The Koran and the teachings of the Prophet were divine revelation, but they are open to modification because even God, or especially God, realized that life is change and while some practices should be immutable, others must change with the times. This revision of practices is called 'Ijtihad.'

He paused.

"The other approach to Islam is 'conventional,' he continued. "It is held by religious extremists, such as members of the Taliban or Al Queda. They have tried to make Pakistan a nation in which their own totalitarian version of Islam would prevail. They are not as interested in Islam as they are in money and power. Today, many religious leaders in Pakistan are as rich as Catholic bishops in Europe at the time of the Reformation. The extremists would not be averse to destroying Pakistan altogether by igniting a civil war between themselves and the moderates."

Elfie began to cough. She had caught a cold on our long flight from Los Angeles.

Justice Iqbal got up and went into another part of the house. He came back with a bottle of cough syrup. He poured some into a spoon and gently fed it to Elfie. Her coughing stopped.

"Has Pakistan failed?" I asked.

"We don't have the failure of a nation," he answered. "We have the failure of a generation which did not bring Pakistan to its promise. Pakistan was the dream of a poet [Muhammad Iqbal]. The dream died at the hands of politicians. The first governor of Pakistan was Muhammad Ali Jinnah, who worked with my father. He died after little more than a year. His successor, Liaquat Ali Khan, was assassinated three years later before he could get Pakistan to agree on a constitution. The people who took over had nothing to do with the Pakistan movement. They were bureaucrats. Politics became based on personalities, not parties."

9

For another and more controversial viewpoint, we went to see Dr. Israr Ahmed. Millions watch him through a popular television program on which he preaches the teachings of the Quran. The program is broadcast on Islamic channels in Pakistan, the Middle East, and Africa.

Elfie and I talked with him in his office in Lahore. He is an imposing man in his seventies, tall and husky, with a neatly-trimmed white beard. He was dressed in a black cloak and a tall black hat. He looked like my vision of an Old Testament prophet.

We sat opposite him at the end of a long table. Two of his sons sat on our right. The office was immaculate. The walls were painted sky blue and lined with orderly bookshelves. It was a sharp contrast to the dusty city outside.

He put down a briefing paper he had been reading when we entered.

"You are a Quaker?" he asked in a deep voice. "What is that?"

"That's not a simple question to answer," I said.

He seemed genuinely curious. I continued.

"Quakerism is a Christian sect started in the mid-1600's," I said. "We have no clergy. We believe that everyone is capable of delivering devotional ministry because the inner light of God resides in everyone, and we seek the immediate experience of God through group meditation."

He looked interested. I tried to relate it to Islam. "In the early 1800's, there was a schism in Quakerism. A New York Quaker named Elias Hicks said he believed Jesus was only an enlightened prophet, not the son of God. The schism was healed when I was a boy, but the Quaker meeting in which I grew up followed Elias Hicks' teachings. I never felt Jesus was actually the son of God. I didn't think it mattered."

"Ah," Dr. Israr said, laughing, "you are a Muslim."

"Maybe, down deep, we all are Muslims or Quakers and everything else," I said.

He turned to Elfie. "Are you a Christian?" he asked.

"Yes, I am," she replied.

"Then you believe in Jesus Christ."

"Yes," she said. "I love what he symbolizes."

"Then you must know that Jesus was never crucified," he answered. "He was taken up to heaven by four angels. It was Judas who was crucified."

"I don't think that would go over well in Rome," Elfie said, smiling.

Dr. Israr looked Elfie in the eyes and shook his head. He seemed disappointed.

I looked at my notes. There were questions I wanted to ask. Dr. Israr had written thoughtful books and pamphlets advocating what Justice Iqbal called a "conventional" approach to Islam. I wanted to know his thoughts on the current antagonism between Islam and the West.

"What can be done to bring East and West together?" I asked.

"Nothing," Dr. Israr answered, "because now the systems are in the grip of the Jews. They are the enemies of Islam and Christianity as well. And the Christians don't know it. Especially the Protestants. They are just tools in the hands of the Zionists."

"The United States was founded on the principle that politics and religion should be separated," I said. "Am I right in believing that Islam believes politics as well as religion are one?"

"That idea of separation came from Europe," he said. "Islam believes that the sovereignty belongs to God, not to human beings. So what comes from the holy prophet is divinely inspired. What he taught will never change. They are fundamentals."

"What about modern technology?" I asked. "Nothing in the Quran mentions that. Television, for example. Is Islam opposed to modern technology?"

"New things we do accept," he replied. "These things are not forbidden. Man has invented them through powers given by God. But it is how they are used. The use of these things has become soiled."

"Is there a feeling that the United States has violated some of the teachings by the way these things are used?" I asked.

"The Islamic reaction to American policies is hatred," Dr. Israr continued. "Hatred toward America. And it is growing day by day. Day by day. Nobody can stop it. The social system has broken down. Western television is already deep into the abyss. Pakistan should sever all connections with the United States. Stop acting as their agents. We should peacefully settle the issues in our area. And then, for the whole of Pakistan, some thought has to be given to the provinces. Let the provinces go by themselves."

"And be run under Islamic law?"

"The difference between Jesus and Muhammad," he said, "was that Jesus did not bring any laws. He revived the religion of Moses, because the Jews were practicing the religion only by the letters. The spirituality had gone out of the Jews, and Jesus made it re-enter into their hearts. Muhammad brought spirituality and law, like Moses."

Elfie interrupted. "I am a Swiss and I was brought up in a Swiss Reformed church. So what you are saying is that Muhammad was part of a continuation from Jesus and Moses and that is why we should have accepted him?"

"Yes," he said. "When you believe in one God and that Jesus was only a messenger, you have to accept the teachings of Muhammad. Jesus showed us love but we betrayed his teachings. Jesus never brought any law. The Gospel doesn't have any law. It has sermons. It has good teachings, moral teachings."

"We in the West also have a concept of individual freedom," I interjected. "Is that in conflict with Islamic law?"

"I believe in freedom," he said. "Freedom of expression, freedom of organization, but within the limits of the Quran and the teachings."

"How would you change society so that it conformed to the teachings of Islam?"

He leaned back. "Only one word," he said. "One word: Revolution."

"With guns and bombs?"

"Yes. You got your freedom from England with guns and bombs. Is that forbidden? You use guns and bombs in Afghanistan." He paused. "But it is not feasible. Instead, today, a mass movement. A peaceful mass movement. What you may call an unarmed revolt. That will change the government system."

"Why don't people who want this kind of peaceful revolution go out and preach the benefits of a better society?" I asked. "Instead of doing what the Taliban is doing, using bombs and assassinations?"

"Preaching by itself never brings about revolution," he replied. "After preaching you have to have a revolutionary party. Strong. Disciplined. And then you have to take on the existing political, social, economic system. A few thousand people can do it. You can't do it by elections. People are overwhelmed by elections. Elections only run the system, not change the system."

"Is someone trying to bring about peaceful change through the teachings of the prophet Muhammad?" I asked.

"Yes," he said. "There is a forum. I founded it."

Dr. Israr had been influenced by Muhammad Iqbal and others while a student at King Edward Medical College in Lahore and when he received a Master's Degree in Islamic studies from the University of Karachi. In 1957, he had set up his own organization to revitalize Islam by propagating the teachings of the Quran in contemporary terms. In 1971, he gave up a thriving medical practice to work full-time for the revival of Islam.

"How are you working to spread Islam?" I asked.

"Through lectures, books, journals, audio cassettes, video cassettes, CD's, all these things."

"How many people are working on this in the United States?"

"Maybe about 200 people. Mostly they work at their own places. Traveling in America is not an easy job. It is a very big country."

"How would you achieve this revolution?"

"First, a new idea has to be flown. First, people have to accept Islam as their religion. For me, the most profound example of the revolutionary process is in the life of Muhammad. He started as a preacher like Jesus but he ended as the head of the state, of no less a country than the Arabian Peninsula, and that was the starting of the exporting of the revolution, east and west and north. Within 24 years it was from Oxus to Atlantic."

"I would assume it would take hundreds of years for world-wide following of Islam?"

"Oh, no. I hope it is not very far. Because the final revelations of St. John are coming to be fulfilled very soon."

"The Apocalypse?"

"Yes. It is not far away. And, before that, in some part of a Muslim country, the Islamic system will be enforced. There is going to be a clash between the Muslims on the one side and the Jews and the Christians on the other. And one of the effects will be the

Armageddon. After that, Jesus will come down. He will come back. And he will be a Muslim. He will be a Muslim. So he will break this cross of yours. He will say, 'I was never crucified. It was Judas who was crucified.[3] What are you doing?' And then Christianity and Islam will become one. And the Jews will be excommunicated."

"Killed?" I asked.

"Killed," he replied.

"Is the war the United States is now fighting against the Taliban part of the Apocalyptic prophecy?"

"It is the starting point."

After we left, Elfie said only one word: "Frightening."

"So far different from Javid Iqbal," I said. "But, in radically different ways, both are seeking the soul of a nation. Javid Iqbal seeks it through thoughtful interpretation of scripture. Dr. Israr seeks it through rigidly following dictates laid down by scripture."

---

3   Author's Note: This Islamic belief is based on the Gospel of St. Barnabus, which was not included in the regular Biblical canon after the Council of Nicea in 325 AD.

10

"People in Lahore like to eat in restaurants," Arshad told us that evening. "We should try one of the food streets."

Shabir drove us a few blocks, past shuttered shops. He parked near an arch spanning the street. Beyond the arch were tables stretching from the store fronts into the street. The street and the tables were crowded, and Elfie stopped every few feet to take photographs.

At one table, a family — grandparents, parents and young children — were eating grilled chicken. Elfie asked if she could take their picture.

"Yes," replied a gray-haired man. "Would you like to sit with us?"

Elfie moved to the end of the table, next to a woman in a white sari. A small boy stood next to her. Someone passed her a plate of chicken.

"No, thank you," she said. "We're just walking."

I took some photographs. Elfie sat for several minutes, holding their baby and talking with the people sitting closest to her.

After several minutes, she stood up. "Thank you," she said. "Enjoy your dinner."

We walked farther down the street, joined now by Shabir. Everywhere, tables projected out into the street from small restaurants. Most served chicken or lamb. Outside one shop, a portly man was frying fish. His pendulous belly seemed ready to droop into a shallow vat of hot grease. In another, a man sliced strips of lamb from a carcass hanging from a hook. In another, a boy carefully watched chickens turning on a rotisserie.

Every time we paused, a waiter invited us to sit down or enter his restaurant.

We walked into a restaurant with a floor of small white tiles and walls covered by red Formica panels.

I looked at Arshad.

"I would suggest grilled chicken, chapattis, and lentils," he said.

I also wanted a Coca-Cola. Elfie wanted tea. Arshad walked to the front of the restaurant and ordered for all four of us.

Another family came in and sat opposite us. We smiled at each other.

"She has a pretty shalwar kameez," Elfie said as the woman sat down. "She is very beautiful."

Elfie held up her camera.

"May I take your picture?" she asked.

I thought it might seem presumptuous. Many Muslim women don't like their picture taken.

The woman smiled. She nodded her head yes. Later, when they were leaving, the woman came to our table and shook Elfie's hand.

We finished eating. The food had been good. We walked some more.

Above the shops and restaurants, the upper stories of the buildings were brightly lighted. The upper floors projected a few feet above the street and were painted in bright colors.

"It's Lahori style of architecture," Arshad said.

Lahore is a night city. People dine late and stay up late. We went to bed early. We were to leave the next morning for Rawalpindi and Islamabad.

11

Elfie surprised me in the morning.

"I will be sad to leave this hotel, and this neighborhood," she said.

"Why?" I asked. "You were so reluctant at first."

"After the initial annoyance of being woken up at all hours of the night, and once I had adjusted to the local time," she said. "I felt rather happy when, at five a.m., the muezzin called to remind us of our prayers. So I thought of all my loved ones, prayed for their well being, and I felt at peace."

Before we left, we went to an office on the roof. I wanted to check my e-mail on the Internet.

"Look at the view," Elfie said, taking me outside. We were five stories above the street. Fruit vendors were pushing carts piled high with bananas and pomegranates into position beside the sidewalk. The air was fragrant with the smell of cinnamon and cloves. Across the street was a jumble of houses with peeling paint. On the roof gardens, women were hanging brightly-colored clothes, children were playing, a cat was prowling. The children waved to Elfie. The women smiled. Yet as soon as I joined Elfie, the women rushed into their houses.

Elfie led me away from the edge. We wove our way through freshly laundered sheets hanging from clotheslines. In an alcove, painted yellow, we saw the hotel's laundry: two small household size electric washing machines, two metal wash tubs, a large gray concrete tub. On the right side was a broken field bed, resting on bricks. On the bed was a pillow, and a blanket. The young laundry-man, wearing a sleeveless white undershirt, was sitting on the edge of the bed.

We smiled at each other. Elfie told the young man she was sorry to have disturbed him. We threaded our way toward the door, passing through more rows of sheets hanging on the line.

12

Before leaving Lahore, we went to the Lahore Central Museum, a Mogul-Gothic-Victorian building built by the British in 1890.

"There's Kim's cannon," I said, looking across the Mall. No ragged small boys were playing on it. The "municipal orders" of Kipling's day had been augmented by a sturdy iron fence. The cannon was not alone. A short way behind it was another symbol of military power: a gray jet fighter plane angled on a pylon as if on take-off. It was pointing east toward India.

The museum had changed since my last visit. "Once," I told Elfie, "I had used a copy of Kim as a guidebook. The museum, the 'wonder house,' was just as Kipling had described it."

I wanted to show Elfie a statue I had seen on my first trip to Pakistan in 1972. It had haunted me ever since. We walked past exhibits of Islamic illustrated manuscripts, rugs, and a collection of Gandharan sculpture until we found it. The statue was of the fasting Buddha. It portrayed a period in the Buddha's life when he was seeking enlightenment by starving himself. He ate only one grain of rice a day. The figure was so emaciated that it was painful to look at.

"It took a woman to get the Buddha to end his fast," I said. "She had come to where he was sitting. She was on her own pilgrimage, to worship a tree deity. Eat, she told the Buddha, like an overbearing mother, and he realized that punishing his body wouldn't get him where he wanted to go. So he began eating again."

"We should leave if we want to make it to Rawalpindi before dark," Arshad said. "We can have lunch on the road."

I wasn't sure what to expect. Would we take the congested Grand Trunk Road?

On my first trip to Pakistan, in 1972, I had been surprised that many of the roads had only one paved lane. The other lane remained dirt.

"Why not pave the whole road?" I had asked.

"It is so that the government can claim to have more miles of paved road than they actually do," I was told.

"Clever," I said.

After leaving the congestion of Lahore, we entered a new motorway. It was called the M-2. It was built by a South Korean company, Dawoo. The old road, the Grand Trunk Highway, was built in 1540 by Sher Shah Suri, an Afghan ruler who wanted to link all of northern India with Kabul. Kipling set most of Kim along the Grand Trunk Road. The M-2 is far different from Kipling's "river of life as nowhere else exists in the world." It is wide and uncluttered and it passes through forests and fields green with farmers' crops.

We reached Rawalpindi in the late afternoon.

Rawalpindi was settled centuries ago as an encampment for the Rawal tribe along a river once noted for its purity. Now the river is little more than a deep ditch, its banks overgrown with weeds, its edges cluttered by industrial buildings and auto repair shops. I remembered Rawalpindi as a varied city: the British built cantonment of large houses and leafy lawns, the bustling Saddar Bazaar where horse-drawn taxis attended by bored looking men waited for passengers, and the sidewalks lined with tables piled high with used American clothing, most of it long out of fashion. I had been curious about the city and spent many hours exploring Rawalpindi on foot. I liked its architectural mix of buildings, its unhurried pace, and its pleasant surprises. One surprise had been a man lying on his belly beside the road while another man walked barefoot on his back giving him a massage.

Now, Rawalpindi was crowded and chaotic, heavy with traffic, almost unrecognizable from my previous visits. The Western press calls it a "garrison city". That is inaccurate. Although there is a military garrison (it was headquarters for the British Northwest Frontier Forces and now for Pakistan's army), it is a vital civilian city.

As we drove through the crowded streets, I thought back to an earlier trip more than ten years before. Saeed had invited me to dinner. It was where we had started a fast friendship.

He had been manager of the Pakistan Tours Limited office at Flashman's Hotel, where I was staying, and I had gone there for advice about traveling to Hunza. We talked for quite a while and, smiling an infectious grin that accentuated the laugh lines around the corners of his eyes, he had invited me to dinner. I accepted and we became friends almost immediately. I started back to my room. The day was hot and I was thirsty. I decided to buy some cold beer. I hadn't had a beer for several weeks, for Pakistan is prohibitionist, but I knew that as a foreigner I would be allowed to buy beer.

The liquor store was a small, white shack on the grounds of Flashman's. It was open for only an hour or so in the afternoon. A dour-faced clerk stood behind a wooden half door, which acted as a barricade. It had no windows; the inside was dark, illuminated only by a single, low-wattage light bulb.

"I'd like to buy some beer," I said. "What kind do you have?"

The clerk looked me over suspiciously. I knew that, except for the ultra-orthodox, Pakistanis are fairly tolerant towards drinking, and that many people buy alcohol from bootleggers. In their poetry, be it in Urdu, Persian, or all the other native languages, there are constant references to "Sagi,' the dispenser of drinks;

"Sharaab," intoxicating drink; "Saaghar," goblet; and various states of intoxication. Still, under the withering eye of the clerk, I felt uncomfortable.

"Murree only," the clerk said. Murree beer was once brewed at the town of Murree, a former British hill station, an hour or so by car from Islamabad. Now, I learned, it is brewed in Rawalpindi, about three miles from the hotel.

"Okay," I said. "Can I have six bottles?" I wanted to keep some in my room as a reserve.

"Your passport?" the clerk asked.

He flipped through the pages, looked at the photograph and then at me, and finally slapped several pages of smudged mimeographed forms on the counter. I looked at them, mystified, and he pulled a page from the top.

"Sign here," he ordered.

I read it. It asked that I certify that I would use the beer only for religious purposes. I signed it.

The clerk checked my signature against the signature in my passport. He looked at the picture again, and then at me. Satisfied, he went to the back of the shack and returned with a large, plain brown corrugated paper box. It held six one liter bottles of Muree beer.

I paid him and carried the box back to my room in both arms, the weight resting against my chest, thinking of religious purposes, of mosques, the pope in Rome and holy communion, of Catholic churches in Chiapas, Mexico, where worshipers drink a strong, clear liquor while sitting on the floor in front of effigies of saints, and of the silent worship of the Quaker meeting in which I had grown up, where Mrs. Parry, the prohibitionist superintendent of the First Day (Sunday) school would stumble over sentences when reading us Dickens' *Christmas Carol*. She was cutting out all references to alcoholic drinks. To justify six liters of beer, I figured I had to do a lot of praying.

A few hours later, Saeed came to pick me up. He brought his son, Adam, who was then about seven years old. Adam was freshly-washed. His black hair was slicked down with water. His face was alight with curiosity. He stood behind the front seat looking out the side window while we drove through the city.

Saeed's house was off what seemed to be a secluded back street. It was one story high with a long, narrow lawn in the front. A couch, chairs, and tables were set up on the edge of the grass.

Adam ran from the car to the house. His mother and two sisters were watching from a front window. Saeed took me to the house and introduced me, but we did not talk. Saeed and I went back to the lawn, and he introduced me to two other guests.

One was Shah Khan, a distinguished man in his sixties. He was Saeed's uncle. Later, I would learn that he was a national hero. As a young man, he had led a force which invaded Kashmir at the time of independence from Great Britain. India and Pakistan are still skirmishing over Kashmir. Shah Khan was a son of Mir Sir Mohammad Nazim Khan, KCIE, who ruled Hunza for thirty-nine years. The other guest was Saleem Akhtar Malik, a brilliant and wise former Army officer, who came from a distinguished family and would become a good friend.

We sat in the garden. Saeed's wife and daughters stayed in the house. The night was hot and humid. Saeed went into the house and returned with three small electric fans and an extension cord. He put the fans on the lawn; they provided some relief from the heat.

We talked about Pakistan, and my plans to go to the northern areas. They told me of the Shandur Polo Tournament, held once a year at the world's highest polo field, a mountain pass 12, 500 feet high in the Hindu Kush Mountains. They told me some of the history of Hunza, the land I had long dreamed of. And then, Saeed went back to the house. He put two small stereo speakers and a small boom box on the window sill and put on a tape of music from

Hunza. Then, he, Shah Khan, and Saleem Malik, showed me how to dance Hunza style. It was graceful and sinuous, with short footwork, elaborate variations on what could be a polka step, and the body and hands moving in the flow of the music. We moved individually, never touching, but synchronizing our steps and movements to the music and to each other.

"Do women dance this way, too?" I asked.

"No," Saeed said. "In Hunza women don't dance with men."

Now, years later, I remembered the evening, and I was looking forward to seeing Saeed again.

In a residential area just beyond the Saddar Bazaar, Shabir turned the car down a leafy street onto a parking area in front of a one-storey house.

Arshad went into the house. He returned with Saeed and a tall young man. Saeed was beaming. The young man was his son Adam, now 22. We all embraced, after the Pakistani custom, and Saeed took Elfie's hands in his own.

"I'm so glad you came," he said.

Then, he turned back to me.

"Remember that house?" Saeed asked. He pointed to a house next door.

"No," I said.

"That's where I used to live, where the party was," he said. "They've built another house in the garden, but that's where I used to live." I did not recognize it.

Elfie, Arshad, Shabir, and I went into Saeed's office. Saeed and I talked enthusiastically, remembering my previous trips and our expeditions to the Northern Areas for the Shandur polo match and fishing in the 1990's.

Saeed showed me a schedule he had prepared for our visit. "I've arranged for you to meet interesting people," he said.

I recognized few of the names, but their descriptions were impressive. I was heartened by the warmth of Saeed's welcome and happy to be back. I was looking forward to seeing Pakistan and old friends again.

When we walked back to the car, Elfie, smiling happily, turned to me. "He treated you like the prodigal son returning. It shows a real bond of friendship from years ago."

It was true. I was pleased.

13

Shabir drove us the eight miles into Islamabad. We had to make a detour. Part of the road and a whole city block were torn up. Billboards announced the site would be a hotel and shopping mall. Behind the billboards was a deep hole in the ground. It took up almost the entire block. Only the hotel lobby had been built. It was strikingly modern and outlined in blue fluorescent lights.

"It will be a thirty-seven storey, seven-star hotel," Shabir said. "It is being built by Dubai people. It will have two residential towers, corporate offices, a five-storey shopping mall, and parking for 2, 000 cars."

"Incredible," I said.

"Yes," Shabir said. "Welcome to Islamabad." He turned to us with a broad grin. "You are now leaving Pakistan."

It seemed we were. Islamabad is unlike the crowded cities elsewhere in Pakistan. It was built in the 1960's to be the capital of Pakistan and to reflect the newest ideas in city planning. We drove down wide streets divided by median strips planted with grass and trees. Large, well-cared-for houses, protected by concrete walls and solid iron gates, lined the streets. One friend calls Islamabad, with sarcasm, "Islamabad the Beautiful."

Shabir took us to the Hunza Embassy Lodge, a guest house on a quiet, tree-lined street. We chose a room with two single beds, a sitting area, TV, refrigerator, and a large green-tiled bathroom. Outside the room was a new computer providing free internet access.

We went to the dining room for dinner.

"What do you suggest?" Elfie asked.

The menu card was in English and I looked at the side listing Chinese food. As I had hoped, the dish I had been waiting to eat was there.

"Chicken Shashlik," I said, "and rice."

Elfie agreed. We both liked it.

14

Taxila is an hour's drive from Islamabad. It was a provincial capital of the Gandharan Kingdom, once the largest kingdom in India. It flourished for 1, 000 years, from about 516 BC to around AD 600. I wanted to go there because of Alexander the Great.

"What did Alexander have to do with Pakistan?" Elfie asked. I had been reading books about Alexander before we left Los Angeles.

"Alexander marched to Taxila in 326 BC.," I explained. "He had wanted to conquer the world and already had taken Arabia and Persia and Afghanistan. Taxila was the first city he planned to conquer in India, which was fabled for its riches. India would mark the end of his conquests. He believed that it lay at the edge of *The Eastern Ocean*, which he had been told surrounded all the world. He planned to use it to take his men and the riches he would steal back to Macedonia.

"Alexander is still remembered in Pakistan," I told Elfie. "Children are named after him. They're called Sikander, the Indian equivalent of Alexander. Many Pakistanis have red hair and claim they are descendants of Alexander's troops. Alexander lingered in Taxila for several months. He made it his headquarters."

"Why Taxila?" Elfie asked.

"The Greeks considered it the greatest of all cities in South Asia. It was a major center of learning. Its universities taught virtually everything: mathematics, law, history, medicine, social sciences, the arts, astronomy, and military tactics. Scholars came from all over. It was a religious center, too. Pilgrims trekked hundreds of miles across China's Taklimakan desert and then walked south along narrow paths scraped out of the arid mountains beside the Indus River. To demonstrate their piety and also, they believed, to ensure their safety, the scholars carved statues and painted pictures of the Buddha in caves all along the route. Some of those paintings and statues are still there. Others have been stolen; many are in museums in the West."

Shabir pulled into the driveway of a stolid, large stone building. It stood at the edge of quiet green fields. Cows grazed contentedly behind low stone walls.

When I first visited it in 1972, Amjad Mahmood Kayani, the museum director, met me at the door. He was short and heavy-set and he had a thin mustache and balding hair. He led me through the museum. I followed the same route with Elfie. Saeed, who had come with us, followed. We started at a relief map of Taxila at the center of the room. It showed models of three mounds, which are all that is left of Taxila's three cities. We walked through the exhibits. Most of them were behind glass cases. They showed artifacts of life in Taxila before the birth of Christ: toy terracotta wagons pulled by animals that looked like hippopotamus, pottery condensers used to purify water, metal or clay cooking pots, metal coins, silver hand mirrors. "Silver was for the rich," I said, remembering what Mr. Kayani had told me. "It was a sophisticated, hierarchical society." We approached the last exhibit. Four teen-age boys were horsing around in front of a glass case display case. A museum guard walked over. "Please settle down," he told them. "You'll give a bad name to Pakistan."

60

We drove to a dirt path that led to an opening in a tall, gray stone wall. Behind the opening was another wall. Hostile invaders trying to enter the city would have to make a sharp turn through a narrow passageway. Behind the walls were the neatly laid out foundations of a small city: a broad main street, narrow side streets, houses with small rooms.

I could imagine Alexander at the wall, in the clear October air, astride his horse, Bucephalus. He would have been in armor and wearing a white tunic, his long blond hair blowing in the wind. He would have been flanked by his elite cavalry, which he called his Companions.

Alexander planned for a big battle. He had expanded his army to 120, 000 men. He had fought bitter battles with hill tribes. When he crossed the border between Afghanistan and India, he was met by letter bearers sent by King Porus (Raja Puru), ruler of the lands between the rivers Hydaspes and Ascines (Jhelum and Chenab) in the Punjab. Alexander read Porus' letter to his troops.

"King Porus of India, to Alexander, who plunders cities: I instruct you to withdraw. What can you, a mere man, achieve against a god? I am invincible: not only am I the king of men, but even of gods...So not only do I advise you. but also I instruct you, to set off for Greece with all speed."[3]

Alexander replied:

"Alexander, to King Porus, greetings: You write to me that you are king of gods and of all men even to the extent of having more power than the gods. But I am engaging in war with a loudmouthed man and an absolute barbarian, not with a god. So the nations I have defeated in war cause you no astonishment and neither do boastful words on your part make me a coward."

Alexander rode eastward. He crossed the Indus above what is now Attock and marched his men across some thirty miles of desert to the plain in front of one of Taxila's walled cities. He lined

---

3   Plutarch of Chaeronea, Life of Alexander the Great, Section Six

up his forces for battle, and he waited for Taxilan troops to surge through the gates to attack.

Only one man walked out. He was King Omphis (known as Taxiles to the Greeks). According to Plutarch, the Greek historian, he had "a realm in India as large as Egypt, with good pasturage, too, and in the highest degree productive of beautiful fruits."

Taxiles knew of Alexander's reputation for merciless warfare. Taxiles, Plutarch wrote, "was a wise man in his way, and after he had greeted Alexander, said: 'Why must we war and fight with one another, Alexander, if thou art not come to rob us of water or of necessary sustenance, the only things for which men of sense are obliged to fight obstinately? As for other wealth and possessions, so-called, if I am thy superior therein, I am ready to confer favours; but if thine inferior, I will not object to thanking you for favours conferred.' At this Alexander was delighted..."

He challenged Taxiles to a battle. It was not to be between their armies. It was a battle to see who could give the most. "So, after receiving many gifts and giving many more," Plutarch wrote, "at last [Alexander] lavished upon [Taxiles] a thousand talents in coined money." (A talent of silver weighed 75 pounds. I figured that in today's money, this would equal about $26, 030, 000, with the value of silver being $1001 per kilogram).

"This conduct greatly vexed Alexander's friends," Putarch wrote, "but it made many of the Barbarians look upon him more kindly."

As a boy, Alexander had been tutored by Aristotle, and he was deeply interested in philosophy. Yogis and holy men fascinated him. Soon after making an ally of Taxiles, Alexander sat down to discuss philosophy with scholars who practiced an asceticism so strict they wore no clothes. No one reported what Alexander wore, but he did throw a large dinner party that evening.

Alexander was not long diverted from his initial mission. Taxiles asked Alexander for help. He wanted to stop Porus and his ally Absares, the King of Kashmir, who ruled the lands beyond the

Hydaspes, including the present city of Lahore. Together they were trying to conquer the whole of Punjab. Would Alexander fight them?

Alexander agreed.

Alexander fought Porus at Jhelum. It was to be Alexander's greatest battle in India. Porus attacked with 20, 000 men and 130 trumpeting, ferocious elephants. Porus, himself, led the final elephant charge. It was a disaster. He lost more than 12, 000 troops. Both his sons were killed. He was captured and brought to Alexander in a cage. Lucius Flavius Arrianus (Arrian), the Greek-born Roman historian, philosopher, and general, who wrote a definitive history of Alexander in the Second Century, AD, described their meeting:

"Alexander, informed of his approach, rode out to meet him, accompanied by a small party of his Companions. When they met, he reined in his horse, and looked at his adversary with admiration: he was a magnificent figure of a man, over seven feet high and of great personal beauty; his bearing had lost none of its pride; his air was of one brave man meeting another, of a king in the presence of a king, with whom he had fought honourably for his kingdom.

"Alexander was the first to speak. 'What,' he said, 'do you wish that I should do with you?'

"'Treat me as a king ought,' Porus is said to have replied.

"'For my part,' said Alexander, pleased by his answer, 'your request shall be granted. But is there not something you would wish for yourself? Ask it.'

"'Everything,' said Porus, 'is contained in this one request.' The dignity of these words gave Alexander even more pleasure, and he restored to Porus his sovereignty over his subjects, adding to his realm other territory of even greater extent."[4]

Alexander would have gone farther into India, but his troops were battle weary. They wanted to return home. They threatened

4   The Landmark Arrian, The Campaigns of Alexander, ed. James Romm, New York; Pantheon Books, 2010; p 221.

to mutiny. Alexander turned back. He made it as far as Babylon. On June 7, 323 BC, he died. Some historians say he died of typhoid fever; others say pneumonia; others say he was poisoned. He was not yet 33 years old.

Taxila remained a great city. Its citizens adopted Greek as the language of commerce and eventually developed a school of art. Gandharan sculpture combines Indian styles with such Western classical elements as the physiognomy of the figures and the heavy folds of the robes.

15

Wah is a few miles west of Taxila. The town, now a city of half a million people, got its name when an Emperor, either Akbar or Shah Jehan (the records are not clear) stopped at a spring on his way to Kashmir. The water was so sweet and pure that he cried, "Wah!" ("Wow!") Later, a large ornamental garden was built there and a town grew up.

Most people would now speed by on the Grand Trunk Road. The town is cluttered and dusty. The water is polluted with high levels of human excrement. Wah's major importance is that it is a place where Pakistan assembles conventional weapons and ammunition.

That was not the reason we were there. At Saeed's suggestion, Kamran Shafi had invited us to lunch. He is a former Army officer and was press secretary to Benazir Bhutto. He writes an acidic, witty, and highly-popular weekly column in the newspaper *Dawn*, one of the two largest-circulation English language newspapers in Pakistan.

Wah is Kamran Shafi's ancestral home. One of his ancestors carried the mortally wounded Brigadier-General John Nicholson, a hero of the two Sikh wars, the first Afghan War and the storming of Delhi during the Sepoy Mutiny, to the bungalow where he died. In appreciation, the British gave his family a large house and the Wah Gardens, which resemble the Shalimar Gardens in Lahore. Another ancestor was Sir Sikander Hayat Khan, the First Chief Minister of United Punjab in the British era, and one of the leaders of the Pakistan independence movement. Shafi's paternal grandfather, Sir Muhammad Shafi, was head of the Muslim League before independence.

Off the main road, we reached a driveway. It ended at the side of a large house. To our right was a field with tall trees shading a pathway to the front door.

Shafi met us and led us into the living room.

Elfie noticed an antique swinging couch on one side of the room. She walked over to it, admiring the intricate carving.

"How beautiful," she said. "May I please take a picture?" she asked.

"Yes," Shafi said.

We sat in the living room and talked. When Shafi announced that lunch was served, he led us into the dining room.

"Pakistan is the only country that tells us what religion we are," Shafi said as we sat down. "On its founding, Pakistan was a moderate, tolerant nation. It changed under President Zia ul Huq, who imposed the most repressive forms of Islam. Now, the country is in a mess."

"Zia, the evil man who started it all," Saeed added.

Zia overthrew Prime Minister Zulfikar Ali Bhutto in a bloodless coup in 1977. He had Bhutto hanged after a trial for ordering the murder of the father of a political opponent.

Butto had begun turning Pakistan into a rigidly Islamist nation. He had banned drinking and had the National Assembly declare the reformist Amadiya sect of Islam to be "non-Muslim".

Zia tightened the screws.

He turned Pakistan's legal system from one based on Anglo-Saxon common law to one based on Sharia law, the ancient moral code and religious law of Islam based on divine revelations set forth in the Quran and on the sayings and examples of conduct set by Mohammad. A major difference from Anglo-Saxon law is that trials are conducted solely by the judge; there is no jury system, no pre-trial discovery, and no cross examination of witnesses.

Zia instituted such draconian punishments as stoning for adultery, chopping off hands or feet for thieves and robbers, and making blasphemy a crime. Blasphemy he broadened to include disrespect for the Prophet Mohammad and other symbols of Islam. He also imposed stringent rules gagging the media to prevent criticism, declared that the Amadiya sect, which claimed a new prophet, could no longer follow Muslim practices, and amended the constitution to give himself absolute power. His Islamization strengthened the hand of religious leaders, mullahs, who were more interested in power than in the spirituality of religion. One of the impediments to modernization today is the stranglehold imposed by a rigid interpretation of religion.

"I supported President Musharraf at first," Shafi continued. "I thought he could break out of the mold. But he has done little. Our infrastructure is deteriorating."

"I had hopes when he first took power," I said. "His speeches were good."

"His problem is that he never follows through," Shafi said. "His handling of the militants' takeover of the Red Mosque in Islamabad was totally wrong. He should have moved when it first started. Instead he waited and 120 people died. In hindsight, I was wrong in supporting a military dictator. A military coup is not the right way to change governments. We are and should be a democracy."

We moved into the dining room. The table was elegantly set. An attractive, gracious woman silently brought in plates of aromatic food: rice, lentils, chicken, flavored by exotic spices, chapatis, and later, for desert, a sweet semolina.

"This chicken is delicious," Elfie said.

"It is my mother's recipe," Shafi said.

"It's wonderful," Elfie said. "The best."

"If you'd like, I'll send you the recipe.

"Would you?" she said. "I would be very pleased to have it."

"I'll e-mail it to you," Shafi said. He later did.

"How do Pakistanis feel about America?" I asked. "In Senate Foreign Relations Committee hearings recently, someone said America uses Pakistan carelessly, like something to be thrown away when it is no longer useful. Is that the way Pakistanis feel?"

"Pakistanis now look on America as an adversary," he said. "U.S. actions have strengthened the Taliban. What it comes down to is that Americans just don't give a damn. The U.S. says 'we have to support our man in Pakistan (Musharraf).' They don't think. They don't realize what that man is doing to the country. Educated people in Pakistan have become very anti-American. America has no credibility."

"And the nuclear weapons?" I asked. "What will happen to them if the Taliban is successful?"

"At this point, we have nothing to worry about."

"Your newspaper columns are very critical of the government," I said. "Is there any attempt to stop you writing?"

"Nothing overt," he said. "Occasionally, I get mysterious telephone calls. No voices, but heavy breathing on the other end of the line. Or just silence with voices in the background to let me know that there is a connection. When I look at the caller I.D., there is no number displayed. Aside from that there have been no threats. I don't worry."

"What would get Pakistan back on track?" I asked.

"We need a free and powerful judiciary, fair and transparent elections, and democracy, power in the hands of the people's representatives."

16

That evening, we had dinner at Saeed's house. It was Elfie's first meeting with Saeed's wife, Showkat, and his daughter Mariam. A young cousin was visiting. After gifts were exchanged, and we had dinner, which Elfie described as "sumptuous and delicious," I joined Saeed and Adam and Shabir in one part of the living room. We talked politics. Elfie sat with Showkat and Miriam in another part.

Later, Elfie enthusiastically told me about her evening with the women.

"I showed them photographs of my family, my home, Los Angeles, and Switzerland," she said. "Showkat does not speak English and I do not speak Burushaskhi, a language I had never heard of until a couple of years ago. Yet we understood each other through signs and touching and lots of laughter and joy. And Mariam translated when necessary. It was a wonderful evening, almost magic, being transferred into another world, another time."

Elfie thought for a moment and added: "I have been given so much love and attention because of your friendships with these wonderful, interesting people. I feel so enriched from this experience here in Pakistan, of being connected at a deeper level, a rare gift in itself and unforgettable. Thank you for convincing me to come with you."

17

The next day, we met with Raja Tridiv Roy, a permanent Federal Minister. He is a Buddhist of the Theravada sect, the oldest form of Buddhism, and hereditary head of the Chakma Tribe, the largest Buddhist population in Bangladesh. Nearly three million Chakmas live in Banglagesh's Chittagon Hills. Before the 1972 war, they were part of Pakistan's east wing.

Raja Roy came to West Pakistan during the war and served as Cabinet Minister for Minorities. Later he was Pakistan's representative to the United Nations, then for many years Ambassador to Argentina.

We talked at his house in Islamabad. The walls were covered with paintings.

Elfie, a fine artist, was immediately attracted. "May I look at the paintings?" she asked.

"Most of them are from Argentina," he said, walking with her.

We sat in the living room. A servant brought tea and sandwiches and subtly-flavored cookies and samosas.

We talked of Pakistan, beginning with the British division of Bengal into two separate provinces to weaken Muslim power in the early years of the Twentieth Century. We talked of

India's independence and of the leaders he had known as a boy. "Mountbatten, the last British governor general, was more interested in getting the most attractive side of his face photographed than he was in the future of South Asia," he said.

I asked him about the Tailban.

"They operate through fear," he said. "They don't have to stand for elections. And, for whatever, for power or for this or that, there has been a lot of encouragement given to these extremists in Pakistan, especially since Zia ul Haq died."

"What can be done?"

"An alternative force to the Taliban has to be built up. The government, at best, has been ambivalent; that's putting it mildly. Once, Pakistan was tolerant of minorities. Now about ninety-nine percent of the population is Muslim."

"In the United States," I said, "many so-called experts are predicting that Pakistan will split into separate provinces."

"That is very difficult to predict," he said. "The unifying factors are weakening, getting more attenuated."

"What will happen if Pakistan breaks apart?"

"There could be any number of courses. It depends who is behind the breakup: the Russians, the Indians, the Americans."

Before we left, he went to another room and brought Elfie a bright red and yellow silk scarf. "This is a Chakma scarf," he said. "Handwoven by tribal artisans."

He showed her a picture of how women in the Chittagon Hills wore scarves. Elfie touched the scarf gently and put it around her shoulder. "Thank you," she said.

She wore it as we left. She looked beautiful. Raja Roy smiled with satisfaction.

18

The Islamabad Club sprawls over 346 lush green acres on the edge of Islamabad near Rawal Lake. The lake is an artificial reservoir. It supplies water for Islamabad and Rawalpindi. The club's members are Islamabad's elite: businessmen, government officials, diplomats. The diplomatic enclave and government offices are nearby. The club was built in the late 1960's. It has the air of a comfortable men's club on London's Pall Mall.

We joined Saleem Malik in the long reception room.

"I wanted to meet you somewhere else," he said, "but this seemed most convenient." Saleem had changed little since we had first met a decade or so before at Saeed's house. He was tall, erect, and had an air of competent dignity. I was delighted to see him again.

I introduced Elfie. We sat on a leather couch against one wall of the room. Saleem sat in a leather arm chair beside us.

I had brought him a present. I opened the envelope and handed him the Loeb two volume edition of Arrian's history of Alexander's campaigns.

"I thought you might enjoy this," I said. "Arrian is the closest to a contemporary account of Alexander's life. He wrote it about 300 years after Alexander's death, but he used sources contemporary with Alexander."

"You gave me another book on Alexander, when you were here before," he said. He thumbed through the pages.

I knew that as a former Army officer, Saleem was a student of Alexander's campaigns.

"Will you inscribe the books?" he asked.

I took out a pen and wrote a brief note mentioning the day we had spent years before looking for the burial place of Bucephalus, Alexander's horse. Bucephalus is part of the Alexander legend. The horse was owned by Alexander's father, King Philip of Macedonia. Plutarch says he was "so very vicious and unmanageable that he reared up when they endeavored to mount him,"[5] and Alexander, then twelve or thirteen years old, watched the stallion and ordered all his handlers away. Alexander approached the horse, calmed him down, and then mounted him. Alexander had noticed that he was scared of shadows. Soon the two were inseparable. Alexander named him Bucephalus because he had a birthmark which resembled an ox's head. Alexander and Bucephalus fought together from Macedonia to India. Bucelphaus died of injuries suffered in the battle against Porus. Alexander, overcome with grief, led the funeral procession himself and buried Bucephalus in a town he founded on the Jhelum River. The town was named Bucephala.

Saleem led us into the dining room, Darbar Hall. Shahid Rehman, a retired Army major, and his wife were waiting for us at a large round table in front of the buffet table.

"I invited the Rehmans," Saleem told Elfie, "because Shauki, my wife, couldn't come and I thought you might like to have another woman present."

Elfie smiled appreciatively. How thoughtful, she thought.

We took plates from the buffet table. Elfie was dying for a fresh green salad. She turned to Saleem. "Would the salad be safe to eat here?" she asked.

---

5   Plutarch; Ibid

"Probably," Saleem said, "but you're not used to Pakistani food yet so you should probably have something easier on your stomach."

She took chicken and vegetables and mango pudding.

Soon she and Mrs. Rehman were deep in conversation. I could hear part of it.

"I'm very busy preparing for the wedding of our daughter, Hannah," Mrs. Rehman said. "November is the month of marriages in Pakistan. Often, we have to attend two or three a day."

"I have a granddaughter named Hannah," Elfie said. She took some photographs from her purse. The women looked at the pictures and smiled contentedly.

"Would you like to attend the wedding?" Mrs. Rehman asked, spontaneously. "It starts on on November 9th. It ends on November 11th. Your presence would honor us."

"Yes," Elfie said joyfully. "We would be delighted to accept." What a gift, she thought, to be part of this experience.

Adam, who had driven us to the club and was sitting next to me, had been looking at Elfie's photographs. "Your granddaughter is beautiful," he said. "Would she exchange e-mails with me?"

"That would be up to her," Elfie said. "But I think it only fair to tell you that she's engaged to a boy in Santa Barbara."

Adam handed the photographs back. He looked disappointed.

Kamran Shafi stopped at our table. "Something is going to happen any day, now," he said.

Adam said, "I hope it is soon. I don't like not knowing." The tension over the political situation was noticeable virtually everywhere we went.

Saleem and I began talking about what was happening in Pakistan. He leaned closer to me. "Once, ninety percent of the people in Pakistan liked the United States," he said. "Now it's only ten percent."

19

Pakistan has an annual economic growth rate of seven to eight percent, among the highest in the world. I wondered why.

Saeed suggested I talk with Murtaza Hashwani, the CEO of the Hashoo Group. It is one of the richest companies in Pakistan. The company was started by Murtaza's father as cotton traders. It now owns hotels, including the Pearl Continental and Marriott Hotels, in Pakistan's major cities. It explores for oil and gas and owns Orient Petroleum International Inc. It has investments in information technology, minerals, ceramics, pharmaceuticals, travel agencies, real estate. It trades in commodities.

Murtaza Hashmani is in his thirties. He was educated in England and in the United States.

"The Prime Minister took over a bankrupt country," he said, referring to Musharraf. "There was no money even to service our debts. But the Prime Minister chose good people, clean, not corrupt. They set the foundation of economic growth. Consistency of government helped, too. In the past, government changed every three years. It was difficult to make long term business decisions. Now, government policies have been very friendly to business. Pakistan is still virgin territory for business. We need power, better infrastructure, technology, oil and gas. And, retail markets are still developing. Seventy percent of the population is under thirty-five. The climate for growth is excellent."

"Political risk?" I asked.

"Risk is the cost of doing business," he said. "But the political risk is low."

20

We left Islamabad for Peshawar the next day. The morning was hot and humid. The Grand Trunk Road was filled with fast moving cars, SUV's, and psychedelically painted trucks and buses. There was one anomaly: an adolescent boy walking on the side of the road, leading two camels loaded with boxes of cargo. He walked erect, proudly. In his left hand he held, rigidly upright, a deep blue tea pot.

"Why?" Elfie asked.

"I don't know," I replied.

The road went through parched, ocher-colored fields and crossed an invisible line between two low hills.

"This is the geographical point where South Asia becomes Central Asia," Arshad said.

We crossed the Indus River, unbound from a straight jacket of mountain canyons in the north and drifting lazily to the Arabian Sea. We were entering the outskirts of Peshawar, about ninety miles from Islamabad.

The side of the road was dotted with small signs. They contained brief homilies which could have been written by the people who stuff Chinese fortune cookies in America: *Health is Wealth;*

Society Builds Man; Don't Put Off 'Till Tomorrow; Future Prospects Bring Present Joys; Time is Money; Drive With Care.

Peshawar sits on a dusty plain some twenty-five miles from the Khyber Pass and the border of Afghanistan. Peshawar is the capital of Pakistan's Northwest Frontier Province,[6] which runs along the Afghan border north to Tajikistan, once part of Soviet Central Asia. Peshawar is a border city whose origins go back into history's forgotten times. It is a city of districts, and now it is heavily infiltrated by Taliban.

I remembered a visit in 1993. The newest part was the British-built cantonment, with tall trees and wide streets, as neat and orderly as a garden suburb. The old city was Central Asian to the core, with narrow two or three-storey buildings and jumbled streets. Some streets were so narrow that they were little more than alleys along pathways, with shops close to the walkways. The old city had bazaars for every need: cloth, baskets, pottery, birds, fruits, vegetables, even story tellers, doctors, and dentists, who advertise their services with large pictures of human teeth. In the jewelry district, portly men, narrow-eyed, suspicious, sat taking the measure of every passer-by. Beside them in tiny shops were well-worn balancing scales and heavy iron safes.

As I was waiting to cross the street, I met a young man who recognized me as an American.

"I am a student," he told me. "I am studying English. I do not like Pakistan. I want to go to the United States."

"Why?" I asked.

"In Pakistan we all work very hard but we get nothing to show for it," he said. "In America, you can work very hard and become rich."

Suddenly, his face clouded with doubt. "But I worry. In America, there are many robbers. They take your jewelry in the bazaar in New York. Here there are no robbers. You are safe in the bazaar."

---

6   In 2010, the area was renamed Khayber Paktoon Khawa.

Interesting what impressions people have, I thought. I wished him luck.

That evening, I had dinner at Salateen, a restaurant on Cinema Road. Two guide books had recommended it. One said it had the "best Pakistani food in Peshawar and [is] famous for its Pathan atmosphere."

A motor rickshaw driver took me there.

"I wait," he said as I got out at the front door.

"No," I answered. "I'll be fine. I don't know how long I'll be here."

"I wait," he said again. "I take you back to hotel."

"No," I said. "You don't need to wait." I didn't like the thought of him possibly missing another fare. He was insistent. I think that he didn't want to risk not getting another fare.

I asked him to have dinner with me. He spoke a little English as we drove through the city. I thought he might be able to tell me something about living in Peshawar. We sat in a high walled booth on the second floor. We ordered chicken tikka. The servings were generous. I tried to make conversation.

"Do you live in Peshawar City?" I asked.

"My brother have jeep," he answered.

"No," I said. "I wondered if you lived in Peshawar."

"My brother have good jeep. What price you pay?"

"I don't need a jeep."

"My brother. He jeep good," he said. "He cheaper and better."

I realized that his English was limited to a hustler's vocabulary. We sat in silence for the rest of the meal. I gave him half of my chicken. He ate only a few pieces of his own portion and none of mine. The bill for the two of us came to about $6 and, when we left, he carefully wrapped the food left on his plate and took it.

21

"Would it be possible to go to Dara Adam Khel?" I had asked Shabir a few days before Elfie and I left for Peshawar.

"Yes," he said. "But we couldn't go in our car. It is too conspicuous. I have a friend who could take us in his car."

"No," Arshad said. "The area is dangerous. It is restricted. You shouldn't go there."

I was disappointed. I wanted Elfie to see it.

Dara Adam Khel is one of the most famous small towns in Pakistan, perhaps in the world. It is twenty-five miles west of Peshawar, in tribal territory, an area controlled not by Pakistan but by the Afridi tribe and subject to ancient tribal law. Pakistan controlled only the road. To the south is Waziristan, a Taliban stronghold. To the north are other sections of the Northwest Frontier Province, which also are Taliban strongholds and which have their own tribal leaders and government.

Col. Sir Robert Warburton, an Anglo-Indian soldier who served as political officer in the Khyber in the late 1800's, described the tribesmen in his memoirs, *Eighteen Years in the Khyber*. His observation still seems relevant:

"The Afridi lad from his earliest childhood," Warburton wrote, *"is taught by the circumstances of his existence and life to distrust all mankind and very often his near relations, heirs to his small plot of land by right of inheritance, are his deadliest enemies. Distrust of all mankind, and readiness to strike the first blow for the safety of his own life, have therefore become the maxims of the Afridi...It took me years to get through this thick crust of mistrust..."* [7]

When I visited Darra in 1993, it was off limits to foreigners. I had to get permission. And I had to have an escort.

Darra is the gun factory for tribesmen in the Northwest Frontier Province. Gun making is the major, if not the only industry in Darra (the Adam Khel denotes a clan of the Afridi tribe, and is used only in formal discussions).

The gun industry began in 1897 when the British made a deal with Pathan tribesmen. The British would allow the tribesmen to make their own guns under two conditions. First, the tribesmen would give the British free access to main highways. Second, the tribesmen would stop stealing guns from British encampments. The British believed the Pathan-made guns would be inferior to their own Lee-Enfields and Martini Henrys. They underestimated the skill of the Pathan tribesmen.

My escort and I parked on the town's one main street. It was lined with open-front stalls.

I stepped out of the car and was met by a volley of gunshots. Some guns made only a popping noise. Others had a deeply authoritative and threatening report. I clung close to the car and looked around to see if I was safe. Men were firing guns from rooftops, from nearby fields, even from the street. The guns were aimed into the sky and toward an open field; no spent bullets would fall on my head.

---

7 Mary Renault, The Nature of Alexander, New York, Pantheon Books, 1975; p191.

A man with a neatly trimmed mustache walked up to me.

"Where are you from?" he asked.

"The U.S.," I answered.

"Would you like to fire a gun?"

"No," I said.

I began walking down the street. Scores of narrow stalls lined each side. In each one, men were making guns. Some were copies of American.45 caliber pistols. Some were copies of Russian Kalashnikov rifles. In one stall, I saw small anti-aircraft guns.

I stopped outside a stall where a heavily-bearded young man was carefully pouring gunpowder into shiny brass casings, then tapping the lead bullet into place with a small hammer. He didn't look up. I walked a few stalls down and went into one of the shops. A man dressed in black shalwar kameez, most of his face covered by a bushy black beard, was sitting on the floor. Beside him were simple tools: a bench vice, metal and wood files, and hammers. Copies of Kalashnikov rifles hung like hunting trophies on the walls.

"Asalam Aleikum," I said.

The man stood. He picked up a rifle.

"I have just finished this one," he said in English.

He handed it to me.

I looked it over carefully. I ran my hand over the wooden stock, which was as smooth and polished as a piece of fine furniture.

"It's beautiful," I said.

He pointed to a rifle lying on the floor. "This is the Russian original," he said. The difference surprised me. His was much better. The Russian stock was rough and unfinished.

"Would you like to fire it?" he asked proudly.

"Thank you. No," I said. I wasn't in the mood. He shrugged his shoulders, and I left the shop.

I walked down to an open field. Aromatic lamb kabobs were cooking on a small grill beside the sidewalk. I bought one and sat on a charpoi under a tree across the street. I ate my kabob hoping that no stray bullets would hit either me or the kabob. My escort joined me. He seemed oblivious to the gunfire.

When we finished, we left for the Khyber Pass. My escort had made arrangements for an armed guard to accompany us. We picked up a thin young soldier at a police checkpoint. He had a mustache and stubble and gentle eyes. He carried a rifle by his right side.

"My name is Hidayatullah Khan," he said as he sat beside me. Those were the only words he spoke.

We went through more check points. Scattered on the hillsides were military forts: Jamrod Fort, Ali Masjid Fort, and Shangai Fort, the regimental headquarters of the Khyber Rifles. Its name was spelled out on freshly white-washed stones.

I was particularly interested. The Khyber Rifles were part of the romance of India.

During British rule, the Rifles was one of eight para-military units, called "Frontier Corps," set up by the British. The Rifles were manned by Afridi tribesmen who served as auxiliaries of the regular British army. Their job was to guard the Khyber Pass. The British writer Talbot Mundy made them the subject of a novel, *King of the Khyber Rifles*. In 1953, the book was made into a movie staring Tyrone Power.

The regimental headquarters is noted for its collection of regimental silver and for maintaining old British Army traditions and ancient Pathan dancing. The dancing is accompanied by regimental musicians playing Scottish bag pipes.

The Rifles' fort is a place distinguished visitors, including Prince Charles and other members of the British Royal Family, have been invited to lunch. I had no invitation, but later, at the Shandur Polo Matches, became friendly with the commandant. Once, he told me, a group of young British naval officers had been invited to lunch. They arrived wearing tee shirts and ragged jeans.

The commandant thought their attire so inappropriate that he wouldn't let them in.

A few miles farther on, we stopped at Landi Kotal, the village closest to the Khyber Pass. It was a collection of two-storey buildings, a rocky main street and a few trees.

"Landi Kotal is a smugglers' town," my escort said. "In the bazaar, you can buy anything you want. Electrical goods, cloth, drugs. Anything."

We settled for tea. We sat on a wooden bench in a small, open sided stall next to a thick tree trunk. Turban clad tribesmen, their eyes full of suspicion, watched every sip we took.

We didn't linger. Down the road, we came to a military check point. A battered, hand-lettered sign propped up against a large rectangular white post warned: "FOREIGNERS NOT ALLOWED BEYOND THIS POST UNLESS SPECIALLY PERMITTED BY THE POLITICAL AGENT KHYBER AGENCY. Our driver stopped the car. Three Pakistan soldiers checked our papers. We drove on.

We came to the last checkpoint and walked up a hill. Beneath us on the right side was a narrow road that snaked through the mountain defile beside a dry riverbed. We were at the Khyber Pass. The name Khyber comes from a Hebrew word meaning "fort". Durani Afghans, once the dominant inhabitants, claim to be "Ben-i-Israel", a tribe carried away captive from Palestine to Media by Nebuchadrezzar, the Babylonian king, six centuries before the birth of Christ.

The British called the Khyber Pass "The Gateway to India." For centuries, it has been the major passageway from Afghanistan through the Spin Ghar Mountains to the Indian Subcontinent.

Great armies have passed through it: Persian hordes under Darius; the troops of Alexander; Ghengis Khan; Timur (Tamberlane), Baber, and the Afghan rulers Nadir Shah and Ahmed Shah Abdali.

The pass was also a major caravan route. Raiding caravans was a major source of income for Afridi tribesmen, and they built many of the forts on the hillsides, ready to swoop down on whoever passed through.

Colonel Warburton described the pass in his memoirs. "...the Khyber Pass, thanks to the quarrels and extractions of the Afridis, was always closed to caravans, trade and travellers, except when some strong man forced them to keep it open.[8]

The British and, more recently, Americans worried that the Russians would use the Pass to invade the Indian Subcontinent.

When we were there, the Pass was empty of traffic. Far in the distance, Torkham, the last town in Pakistan, rested serenely under a gauze of haze. Little romance was left. The Khyber Pass was just a narrow twisting road.

We headed back to Peshawar and stopped for lunch. Opposite the restaurant, a glass display case outside a shop held sex aids: vials of testosterone, and creams called "Raging Bull," "Bear," "Fire and Ice".

---

8   Renault, op cit, p190

22

Before Elfie and I left Islamabad, we had decided to stay at a hotel on the eastern edge of Peshawar. It had been recommended by Dr. Betsy Emerick, a retired college dean and a member of the Orange Grove Friends (Quaker) meeting in Pasadena. Dr. Emerick had visited Pakistan periodically for the Afghan Refugee Girls' schools, which we wanted to visit.

We arrived late in the afternoon. To Elfie and me, everything seemed normal. Pedestrians filled the sidewalk. Brightly colored sheets hung to dry from lines strung in front of stores and apartments. Vendors selling baked goods, fruits, and nuts lined the sidewalks.

Shabir parked the car inside the hotel garage. Arshad seemed uncomfortable. He suggested another hotel. He gave us no specific reason and Elfie insisted on staying at Betsy's hotel. Arshad took us to the reception desk and introduced us to the manager.

"May we go up and see the rooftop restaurant?" Elfie asked. "A friend in Los Angeles recommended it."

Arshad went with us. The manager stayed at his desk to finish some paperwork.

The restaurant had captivated Betsy. "It's lively, with good Pakistani music and good food," she had told us. But it was closed. A black tarpaulin covered the bandstand. Tables were pushed against a wall. We looked over the wall.

"This view is fascinating," Elfie said.

Below us, atop a two-storey building across the street, a small rooftop restaurant was full of men silently eating at tables under a blue awning. Arshad seemed nervous. He rushed us downstairs and then went to the garage to talk with Shabir. The manager showed us several rooms. We were about to pick one when Arshad returned. He pulled us aside. His face was grim.

"We should find another hotel," he said.

"Why?" Elfie asked. "This is an interesting place."

"The service is not good," he said.

Elfie shrugged her shoulders "Our friend in Los Angeles liked it and was always satisfied," she said.

Arshad turned to me. "We should find another hotel," he said.

"Why?" I asked.

"This is not a good place. We should get out of here as fast as possible."

Puzzled, we climbed back into the car. Shabir drove us to another hotel. The rooms were lined up along an inside balcony. They had no exterior windows, and they were dark.

"I don't like this place, Elfie said. "It is too depressing."

"Let's find something else," I told Arshad. "Are there any guest houses?"

We drove to a residential district. It was called University Town. Large houses sat behind thick walls. Several had been converted to guest houses. We chose one that had large rooms and an air of what decorating magazines call "shabby gentility." It had once been an elegant private house. In the entry hall, beside the reception desk, was a photograph of Muhammad Iqbal. He had been a friend of the owners and had stayed there in the 1930's.

We chose a room opening onto a wide balcony which faced the street.

We went back to the dining room, and sat at a long table. A waiter brought us tea.

"I like this place," Elfie said. "But what was wrong with the first one?"

"It was not safe," Arshad said. "We were surrounded by Taliban. We could easily have been a target."

"Okay," Elfie said. "I would not have insisted on the first hotel, if you had told us earlier that it was in such a dangerous location. Everybody understands that."

He didn't answer.

"Do you think I am too outspoken?" she asked. "Too Western?"

Neither Arshad nor Shabir answered, but Shabir's eyes twinkled, and I could see that he was repressing a smile.

Elfie and I went to our room. A few minutes later, Arshad knocked on the door.

"Someone is here to see you," he said.

We hadn't expected a visitor. Arshad nodded toward a man standing in the lobby. He was in his mid-thirties, neatly dressed in a crocheted cap and a gray pin-stripped vest, unbuttoned, over light gray shalwar kameese. He had a neatly trimmed beard and a warm smile. I went down the stairs to meet him.

"I am Ramatullah Rahimi," he said. "I am head teacher at the school for Afghan Refugee Girls."

I was puzzled that he knew we were there. We had hoped that our visit would be a surprise so that we could see the school informally.

"I called him for directions to the school tomorrow," Arshad explained. The school was part of an Afghan refugee camp at a town called Akora Khattak an hour or so back on the GTR.

We sat opposite each other at a long table in the dining room.

"How long have you been in Pakistan?" I asked.

"I came from Afghanistan, from Kabul, twenty-three years ago," he said. "I was twelve years old. The Russians had attacked. My whole family came, except my father and grandmother. It took three days. We walked across the mountains. Some of the children were carried in backpacks. I carried a rifle on my shoulder.

"First, we went to a refugee camp, Kehargra, then to another one at Akora Khattak, where I am now," Ramathullah continued. "No human beings were living there; it was an open field. We registered, slept in tents, and were given Russian passports. The Pakistan government took a census so that they could provide food, blankets, and other things we needed. I grew up in the camp. At first, I worked with a subcontractor building houses in the camp. My family had always emphasized the importance of education and I learned English and learned to be a teacher and started a school for girls. We had fifteen girls to start. I wanted to educate more girls. That's when I met Joe Franko. He offered to help."

Joe Franko was then head of the American Friends Service Committee's western regional office in Los Angeles. He is a mathematician and college professor. He had gone to Pakistan with Edith Cole, the retired school psychologist and member of Claremont Friends Meeting outside of Los Angeles, whose daughter Sarah had married Arif Zaman, the college professor we had visited in Lahore.

"Edith and I were looking for a way to help Afghan refugees fleeing their country after the American bombing in October 2001," Franko told us before Elfie and I left for Pakistan. The bombings in Afghanistan followed the attacks on New York City and Washington, DC, on September 11, 2001.

"We were horrified by what was happening in the world," Franko said. "The refugees were completely innocent people. We felt impelled to follow the words of William Penn, to 'Let us see what love can do.'"

"I wanted to show that Americans could do more than drop bombs," Edith later told Elfie and me. Elfie had been pleased to discover that Edith's father was born in Glarus, Switzerland, where Elfie had been born and grown up, and that Edith's maiden name was Tschudi, a patrician name of that Canton and also the name of Elfie's paternal great grandmother. Edith grew up in St. Gallen.

We finished our tea with Ramatullah and agreed to meet again at the school.

23

"I thought you might like to see some of the history of Peshawar," Dr. Ali Jan said that evening. "I have some slides I've taken of old buildings and tombs."

Dr. Jan is an amateur historian in his late twenties. He invited us to dinner at his parents' house, where he was living while waiting for an American visa so that he could study psychoanalysis at Harvard. He had set up a television and DVD player in the living room.

He turned on the TV. "Peshawar is like nothing else in Pakistan," he said. "The city is more than 2, 000 years old. It is one of the world's oldest living cities, and once was the seventh most populous city in the world. It has always been a frontier settlement. It's a place where the Occident met the Orient. It is a polyglot city. It has people from all over South and Central Asia and the Middle East."

Pictures of ruined buildings and archaeological excavations came on the TV screen.

"Peshawar has had almost as many names as it has had rulers," Dr. Jan continued. "When it was the capital of the Gandharan Kingdom, it was called Gandhara. When the Emperor Baber passed through in his march from Afghanistan to Delhi to overthrow the Lodhi rulers of North India and start the Mogul Dynasty, it was called Begam. Baber was enchanted by the profusion of blooming lotus flowers and changed the name to Pushpapura, the city of flowers. In 1530, his grandson, the Emperor Akbar, gave it the name Peshawar, which means "The Place at the Frontier."

"Until the mid-1950s," Dr Jan explained, "Peshawar was enclosed by a city wall which had sixteen gates. But most of the wall has been taken down as the city has had to expand because of population explosion."

We looked at pictures of ancient city gates and fragments of the city wall.

"Peshawar was once a trading post for caravans from Central Asia, Kabul, Bukhara, and Samarkand," Dr. Jan continued. "It was full of traveling merchants. They sold heavy wool, delicate silks, brilliant dyes, gold thread, fruits, precious stones, carpets. Peshawar also has been an entry point for invading armies and a military headquarters for those who would repel them."

The screen showed a picture of the large fort which dominates the center of the city.

"Now," he continued, "Peshawar is important because it is the link between Pakistan and Afghanistan. It is also the regional center for Pashtun culture, and the cross roads of the struggle between the Taliban and the moderates."

I thought of the difference from the Peshawar I had first known in the 1980's. Now, the city had a different atmosphere. It felt much more intense. Practically all the women were wearing burkas, which gave the city a heaviness, a feeling of fearful anticipation.

A distinguished man in his mid-sixties entered the room. He was Dr. Jan's father, a retired Army officer.

"Would you like to join my wife and me for dinner?" he asked.

Dr. Jan turned off the TV. Elfie, Arshad, Shabir, and I went into the dining room.

Mrs Jan, a stunningly beautiful woman, was standing beside the table, elegantly set with fine china and silverware. She asked us to sit down.

"I thought you might like some of our regional dishes," she said.

A silent young man brought serving plates to the table. Piled high were chicken and mutton and beef patties rich with herbs, vegetables, saffron rice. For dessert, we had dates, pomegranates, and a mango pudding.

We talked late into the evening and returned to our guest house warmed by the unexpected hospitality.

24

Early the next morning the telephone in our room rang.

"You have a visitor," a voice announced.

We dressed quickly and went downstairs.

A young man was waiting in the reception room.

"I am Sharin," he said. "I spoke with Dr. Emerick in Los Angeles this morning. She said you were here. I have jewelry to sell."

Betsy Emerick had told us, "You should buy jewelry from Sharin whom you'll find at the North West Heritage Hotel," she had e-mailed. "More likely he'll find you!"

He had.

We agreed to buy some jewelry for resale at fund raising events for the girls' school. He left and returned as we finished breakfast. He sat opposite us at the long dining room table and unwrapped a small cloth bundle.

The jewels were semi-precious stones, many set in silver. Elfie looked them over carefully. She had a good eye, and she selected several earrings, pins, necklaces, rings, and bracelets.

I discovered her passion for stones years before when I had given her a piece of jade I had found in the sands of the Taklimakan

Desert in Western China. She had been more excited than if I had given her a large diamond ring.

After Sharin left, Shabir and Arshad drove us to a shop, Zardozi, a few blocks from the guest house. The shop sold handicrafts made by Afghan artisans in Afghanistan and in Pakistan. Display shelves lined the walls and ran down in the middle. An Afghani woman stood behind a counter. She welcomed us with a warm smile and did not pressure us to buy.

Elfie picked out embroidered bags, pillow covers, checkbook holders, cell phone holders, wallets, eyeglass cases, key fobs, wall hangings.

"These are beautiful," she said. "They will do well at a fund-raiser in Los Angeles."

We had one more stop to make.

Nasir Azam Sahibzada is program assistant at the United Nations High Commissioner for Refugees regional office in Peshawar. He serves on the three man local committee which oversees the Girls' schools. We needed his permission to visit the refugee camp. We met in his office at the back of a wooden building not far from our guest house.

"How many refugees are in Pakistan now?" I asked him after tea was served.

"We believe four million Afghans fled to Pakistan," he said. "The exact number is unknown. Many Afghans feared that registration was a way to deport them. We believe there are about 2.5 million now in Pakistan. The UNHCR, our office, gives them technical grants and ID cards. The UN is helping to fund relief efforts."

"Are many returning to Afghanistan, now?" Elfie asked.

"No," he said. "Pakistan offers much that Afghanistan no longer can offer. In Afghanistan there is no housing and a lot of relief money is taken by ex-warlords, bureaucrats, or the office managers of contractors. One attraction here in Pakistan is education. The UN is running 150 schools, with 60, 000 students. Our biggest problem is that most parents have no understanding of education. They do not support it. There also is a shortage of female teachers. The student drop-out rate is high. After five or six years of education, many Afghanis leave school."

We finished our tea and thanked him as he handed us a permit to visit the school. It had a limit: We could stay for no more than ninety minutes.

"You saw us on such short notice," Elfie said as we turned to leave. "It feels like you were waiting for us. How could you see us so quickly?"

Nasir looked directly at her. "Don't you think that we know where you are all the time?" he replied. "Two Americans suddenly in this area?"

"I didn't see anyone following us," Elfie said.

"No," he replied, holding up his cell phone. "but the police keep up while you pass through. It's for your own security."

25

The town of Akora Khattak is not listed in the standard guidebooks. You could easily pass through it without thought; just the familiar row of open front shops and dusty streets. But it has more: a Pakistan Tobacco Company factory, which makes Marlboro cigarettes, and Dar-Ul-Uloom, the second largest mosque in Pakistan.

The mosque houses one of the oldest madrassas in Pakistan. The madrassa was founded in 1947. It is one of the largest and most militantly anti-American schools in Pakistan. The formal curriculum is simple: rote memorization of the Quran in Arabic, a language the students do not understand. The madrassa has some 3, 000 students. All are boys. Many have joined the Taliban. One former student is Mullah Omar, the Afghan Taliban leader. The madrassa has been called the Harvard of the Taliban movement. It is also known as Jihad University.

On the edge of Akora Khattak, Shabir turned off the Grand Trunk Road and made a sharp U-turn around the gas pumps at a CNG gas station. He drove down a steep hillside onto a dry riverbed, littered with huge rocks.

"This is a better way," he explained. "It avoids the security checks."

We came to a mud-walled building high on the river bank. It was the first of the Afghan refugee girls' schools, Zarghuna Ana. The high wooden gates opened as we approached. Arshad had called Ramathullah on his cell phone.

The girls were standing in two long rows facing each other in the packed dirt courtyard. They were dressed in immaculate uniforms, black shalwar kameez with long white head scarves. Some held a garland of orange marigolds. Others held marigold petals to throw at our feet. They began softly singing a song of welcome. It was an Urdu poem written by Muhammad Iqbal and set to music. We didn't need to understand the words. The joy on the girls' faces was translation enough.

We walked down the row. Elfie went on the right. I went on the left. We shook hands and bowed as each girl put a garland of flowers around our necks.

The girls walked back to their classrooms. They left their pastel-colored plastic sandals in orderly rows beside a cement walkway beneath a thatched roof arcade. The classrooms were small. The walls were whitewashed rough stone. The floor was packed dirt covered by strips of carpet on which the girls sat, holding small blackboards. Each classroom had one open window, sheltered by the arcade. The window provided the only light. The classrooms had no electricity.

Ramathullah led Elfie through a doorway painted lapis blue and into a classroom for students in the fourth grade. I tried to enter, but the teacher turned her face to the wall so that I, an unknown man, could not see her. I went outside and joined Arshad on the veranda. Arshad used Elfie's camera to take some pictures. Some of the girls covered their faces with their books or small, hand-held blackboards.

Ramathullah introduced Elfie.

"We think about you all the time, about how we can help you," Elfie told the girls. "You have many friends in America. We want you to get a good education."

The girls smiled as the teacher translated.

Elfie asked the girls questions. The girls asked her questions. She told them stories of her own school days and of growing up in Switzerland.

The girls giggled. When Elfie finished, they crowded around her and exchanged hugs.

In another classroom, some older girls spoke a little English.

One pointed to a classmate who had been sitting, shyly observing.

"She is going to be married," the first girl said. "She does not want to."

"What?" Elfie exclaimed. She turned to the prospective bride. "How old are you?"

"Fifteen," the girl replied.

Elfie turned to Ramathullah.

"Fifteen?" Elfie asked. "Don't tell me she is promised to some old man." Elfie thought of the films she had seen and books she had read about child brides and their abominable treatment by in-laws.

"No, no," Ramathullah said, "he is a nice young boy,"

"But she is so young."

"It is our custom," Ramathullah explained. "It used to be that girls married at thirteen. Now, going to school gives them a couple of extra years, which gives their children a better chance to be healthy."

"But where do they go from here?" Elfie asked. "Can they learn a trade? Or go to school? Or do they just become wives and mothers at such young ages?"

She was deeply concerned. She took off her gold bracelet and handed it to the girl. "If you are a bride, engaged to be married," she said, "I'd like to give you a gift."

The girl smiled shyly and, looking stunned, took the bracelet.

Elfie left the classroom. A dozen women, mothers of the students, invited Elfie to talk with them. They went into a dark classroom. I was not allowed in.

"May I take a picture?" Elfie asked.

"No, please. Absolutely not."

Soon, I could hear laughter.

"What were you laughing about?" I later asked.

"They asked me how many children I had," she said. "I told them three, (a daughter and two stepsons) and they asked me what was wrong with me. Was I not well? They told me proudly that they had ten children, seven, six."

"That's a lot," I said.

"Of course," Elfie continued. "They all looked aged beyond their years. I told them that in America we do not have so many children because living and education is very expensive."

"The women," Elfie continued, "told me that they would like to do handicrafts for direct sales to become more independent. I suggested sewing machines and a teacher and I promised to bring it up at the first school committee meeting in Los Angeles."

"Would you like to see the other school?" Ramathulla asked. "The two schools are the only ones that educate girls. The town has 10, 000 families. Custom dictates that Afghan women do not travel far from home."

We climbed back into the car and drove a few hundred yards to another building. Shabir parked in front of a doorway between two high mud brick walls. A blue and gold sign atop the doorway read "Nazu Ana." In smaller letters, it said, "Supported by the Friends Committee (Quakers)." The small letters reflected Quaker modesty. I recalled something Edith Cole had said after the school was established. "We didn't want to shove the Bible down their throats. That's not our understanding of how God works."

"What do the school names, Zarghuna Ana and Nazu Ana, mean?" I asked Ramathullah while Elfie visited more classrooms.

"Ana is Pashtu for mother," he said. "They were two famous Afghan women. Nazu Ana's son was called the grandfather of Afghanistan."

We drove back to the first school. Ramathullah led us into a large room. A desk and an elderly computer sat by the door. On the floor was a brown cloth with neatly arranged serving platters piled high with chicken, rice, and vegetables.

"We hadn't expected lunch," I said.

Ramathullah handed Elfie a plate. Arshad, Shabir, and I took our own plates.

I sat at the table and ate several fork-fulls. I looked up at Ramathullah.

"This food is excellent," I said. "I really like the subtle blend of flavors."

"It is Afghani," Ramathullah said, proudly.

We went outside. The girls were leaving the school, walking in single file.

"They are so beautiful," Elfie told Ramathullah. "I'd like to take one or two home with me."

"Take those two," he said, pointing. "They are mine."

"Oh, you'd miss them."

"Take them," he said with a warm smile. "I have ten."

"Your wife must always be pregnant," Elfie said.

"I have two wives," he answered.

We were silent as we drove back to the Grand Trunk Road toward Islamabad. Finally, Elfie said, "I am deeply touched by this visit. I am moved. The openness and curiosity, the sharing by the women. Their hopes, their fears. Regardless of outer circumstances, we all wish for the same: a healthy family, shelter, and enough to eat."

26

The next morning, Saeed and Salim wanted to talk with me about Pakistan's history. I invited Elfie to join us.

"I'd like to have some time of my own," she said. "I want to catch up on my journal."

"You had better stay here," Saleem said. "It would be unwise to go outside the garden on your own."

Elfie felt restless from the lack of exercise. That morning, she started to run back and forth in the garden, to the amazement of the whole guest house staff.

"I can stay with her," Shabir said. "I can take her wherever she might like to go."

Saleem, Saeed, and I sat in the garden and talked.

An hour or so later, Elfie and Shabir came down.

"We're going out to lunch," Elfie said.

When she returned, she told us: "We went to an Italian restaurant. I was overjoyed. I had pasta. I'm tired of mutton. I know mutton is considered the finest meat in Pakistan, but I think I knew I had had enough when my breakfast eggs started to smell of mutton fat. And, after lunch, Shabir took me to a Western market. I bought some Emmentaler cheese, some Lindt chocolate, some English cookies, peanut butter, cereal, fresh oranges, and kiwis. And, I saw Kamran Shafi. He was sitting with two men at a table outside the market drinking tea. He invited me to sit with them, but I didn't want to interrupt their conversation. I did tell him I was glad to see him because he was the only person I recognized as having actually met before in Pakistan and could say hello to. He laughed."

Elfie and Shabir went up to our room. Saeed and Saleem and I continued to talk.

"I wrote in my journal," Elfie told me later, "and Shabir sat in a chair beside the table cracking open walnuts for both of us. He is a wonderful young man."

27

The next morning, we packed to drive up the Karakoram Highway to Gilgit and to Hunza. Elfie's eyes were bright with excitement. She had been interested since we had first met and I had told her about the mountains, the customs, the history, and the people I had met there.

"We should have our wedding in Hunza," I had told her when we became engaged.

"Where's that?" she had asked.

"In the Karakorams, the Northern Areas of Pakistan," I explained. "It's magical."

Every area has its own legends and customs. I had found Hunza and the Northern Areas the most interesting. We went there to give Elfie a feel of another part of Pakistan, for what I had told Elfie had been reinforced by Elizabeth Lorimer's recounting of her months there in the mid-1930's.

"Hunza has changed a lot," I told Elfie before we left Los Angeles. "Once, it could have been legitimately called a Shangri-La. People co-operated with each other, rather than competed. It was a remote, almost virtually self-sufficient area. The KKH made it accessible and it isn't the way it was in 1935. But you ought to see it. It's part of the richness of Pakistan."

"And you still have some friends there?" she asked.

"Yes, and I'd like you to meet some of them," I replied.

We finished breakfast. Elfie looked toward the door as Shabir entered. We followed him to the driveway. An elegant, thin, gray haired man with plastic-framed eyeglasses was shifting luggage in the SUV.

"This is my cousin, Berham," Shabir said, introducing us. "He's Saeed's cousin, too. Arshad couldn't come. He may be going to a tourism conference in London."

"I need to go to Gilgit," Berham explained. "I'm having a dispute with my brothers over some land. They think I shouldn't inherit it because I live in Paris, and I married a French woman."

"Will we go through Swat?" I asked as Shabir backed out of the driveway.

"No," he said. "Swat is becoming a Taliban area. It is too dangerous. The Taliban are moving into the center of Pakistan from the Afghan border areas. The Taliban are trying to destabilize it. They are killing political leaders and villagers. People are fleeing. Musharraf has not stopped them."

Earlier, at a dinner party in Islamabad, I had met a member of the Swat royal family. His grandfather's grandfather was the Akond of Swat. Edward Lear, the Victorian era nonsense poet, had written a long poem about him. It began:

"Who, or why, or which, or what,
Is the Akond of SWAT?"
Is he tall or short, or dark or fair?
Does he sit on a stool or a sofa or a chair
Or SQUAT,
The Akond of Swat?"

In fact, the Akond was a respected Sufi teacher. The British had installed him as area chief to bring order to the tribal lands.

"Swat is one of Pakistan's most beautiful areas," I told Elfie as we reached the street. "It has been called the Switzerland of Pakistan. It has green Alpine meadows, beautiful rivers, jagged mountains in the background. It also has an interesting history. It was once dotted with Buddhist monasteries and, on its western edges, it was an area the British fought to control in their efforts to keep the Russians out of India."

I was disappointed that we would not pass a small fort called Churchill Picket. It was named after a young British cavalry officer who fought in his first battle there. He later went on to become Prime Minister of the United Kingdom during World War II. He is one of the great men of the Twentieth Century. He was Winston Churchill.

28

In 1897, Winston Churchill was a twenty-two year old subaltern (lieutenant) in The Malakan Field Force under Major General Sir Blindon Blood, K.C.B.

Gen. Blood commanded what Churchill described as "an episode of Frontier War" against Pathan tribesmen. It was one of many battles the British fought to control India. It raged over part of western India, now Pakistan, near the Afghan border. The fighting was brutal and relentless. Losses on both sides were high. Today, it seems a minor skirmish in what is now almost-forgotten history. Yet it is still relevant. Churchill, with great prescience, later looked back on the battle against what he called "militant Mohemmedanism' and offered a prescription for ending the conflict between the tribesmen and the British. Although somewhat simplistic, it could apply, more than 100 years later, as we fight militants in Afghanistan who use the border areas of Pakistan as a base.

"It would seem that silver makes a better weapon than steel," Churchill wrote. "A system of subsidies must tend to improve our relations with the tribes, enlist their efforts on the side of law and order, and by increasing their wealth, lessen their barbarism." [9]

The campaign had a long-lasting effect, at least on Churchill himself. While serving with the Malakan Field Force, Churchill learned to drink Scotch whiskey. The story of how he acquired a taste for Scotch had appealed to me, for Scotch has always been my favorite liquor. Churchill shared the Army's disapproval of those who drank to excess, but to temper the effects of India's sweltering summers while waiting for Gen. Blood to return from an expedition, Churchill, who later earned a reputation as a steady imbiber, learned to drink whiskey. He describes it in *A Roving Commission*:

While waiting, he wrote, *"I acquired an entirely new faculty. I had never been able to drink whisky. I disliked the flavour intensely. I could not understand how so many of my brother officers were so often calling for a whisky and soda. I liked wine, both red and white, and especially champagne; and on very special occasions I could even drink a small glass of brandy. But this smoky-tasting whisky I had never been able to face. I now found myself in heat which, though I stood it personally fairly well, was terrific, for five whole days and with absolutely nothing to drink, apart from tea, except tepid water with whisky. Faced with these alternatives I 'grasped the larger hope.' ... By the end of these five days, I had completely overcome my repugnance to the taste of whisky. Nor was this a momentary acquirement. On the contrary the ground I gained in those days I have firmly entrenched, and held throughout my whole life. Once one got the knack of it, the very repulsion from the flavour*

---

9   Winston S. Churchill, The Story of the Malakan Field Force, London, Longmans & Green, 1988. I've used the reprint issued by 29 Books, Brooklyn, NY, 2004; p 216.

developed an attraction of its own; and to this day although I have always practiced true temperance, I have never shrunk when the occasion warranted it from the main basic standing refreshment of the white officer in the East."[10]

---

10   Churchill, A Roving Commission, New York, Charles Scribner's Sons, 1930; p126.

29

"Why did you move to Paris?" I asked Berham as we headed toward the KKH.

"When I was young," he answered, "a French doctor came to Hunza, trying to find out why people in Hunza were supposed to live to extreme old ages, into their 100's. He wanted to sell medicines to extend life in the West. I agreed to help him. I went back to Paris with him. But we found that people in Hunza didn't live to extreme old age. So we never sold Hunza products."

"Other people do," I said. "you can buy all sorts of Hunza diet stuff on the Internet."

"It doesn't work," he said.

The Karakoram Highway starts just north of Islamabad. I had lost count of the number of times I had traveled it. I think at least six. Shabir told us he sometimes drove it four times a week.

"I once thought the KKH was so exotic," I told Elfie. "A paved road into one of the most impenetrable areas on earth, through the most remote and spectacular parts of Pakistan, the deep gorge of the Indus River on one side, and a panorama of some of the world's highest and spectacular mountains on the other. It's an engineering marvel, carved out of fragile, landslide-prone mountains."

The KKH replaced a narrow, rocky path. The path was barely wide enough for a man on horseback. It wasn't until 1931 that an automobile had even tried to use it. That summer, a French expedition, sponsored by The National Geographic Society, set out to drive across remote areas of Central Asia. Their vehicles were vintage half-tracks, built for service in the French Army during World War I.

The journey through Hunza, the society reported in its monthly magazine,[11] "presented greater hardships and perils than any other portion of the scientific Expedition's route. The resourceful leader of the party, M. Georges-Marie Haardt, succeeded in piloting two of his tractor motor cars over snow blocked passes and across trails which had been obliterated by avalanches to regions never before reached on wheels."[12]

In 1965, nearly two decades after the creation of Pakistan, the Pakistan government decided to replace the pathway with a two-lane paved highway, strong enough for heavy trucks and buses. It would run from Islamabad up to the 16, 500 foot Kunjerab Pass, on the border of China. It would be the highest paved road in the world. It would join a Chinese highway and go deep into Xingjiang along the western edge of the treacherous Taklamakan Desert. It would pass through the city of Kashgar to Urumqui, where it would join with a railhead to Beijing. For the first time since the Silk Route had flourished from the Second to the Eighth Centuries AD, Central Asia would be linked with Pakistan and the Arabian Sea.

With Chinese help, the road was finished in 1986. It opened Pakistan's north to trade and tourism. It consolidated

11 Maynard Owen Williams, First Over the Roof of the World by Motor, The National Geographic Magazine, Vol. LXI, Number Three, (March 1932), pp 320-363.
12 Ibid.

Pakistan's hold on the Northern Areas, which India still claimed as part of Kashmir. And, if war broke out between India and Pakistan, the Chinese could use it to deliver military supplies.

"It's an unpredictable road," I told Elfie. "Many times I have had to wait for road crews to clear a landslide. Once, after a Shandur polo match, I had to wait in Gilgit more than a week. A lot of people were stranded. But it was fun. The people were interesting and we explored some beautiful back country."

Today, the KKH is full of potholes. Long stretches of pavement are missing. The Chinese government is now widening the road. They will use 300, 000 men, demolition experts, and earth moving equipment, which they'll bring from Xingjiang. They will make the KKH a six lane, modern road. They will build a railroad from Kashgar. It will be a massive undertaking. It will take three years. It will allow the Chinese to export more goods from Xingjiang. It is part of China's heavy investment in Pakistan.

A few hours after leaving Islamabad, Elfie and I reached Abbottabad, 4, 000 feet above sea level. Guidebooks say it is pleasantly cool when the plains bake in summer, that it is a popular tourist resort, and that it is the gateway to other resort areas. It also is known as the "City of Schools." Among them is the Pakistan Military Academy, the West Point of Pakistan.

Abbottabad had been a British military garrison, headquarters of the Second Division of the Northern Army Corps. It was named for Major James Abbott, a hero of the Sikh wars of the 1840's. The people of Hazara held him in high affection. His successor named the garrison town after him.

We reached the northern edge of the city. The streets, which had been full of students in blue uniforms, were now almost empty.

"Should we stop for lunch here?" Berham asked.

"Yes," I said. It was after two o'clock.

Shabir drove slowly past several restaurants.

"None of these look very good," I said.

Berham said something to Shabir in Urdu. Shabir made a U-turn. A few blocks later, he pulled the car onto the sidewalk in front of a sand-colored building with a large plate glass window.

"We can eat here," Berham said. It was a department store. One side was marked by a familiar red and white sign, a picture of a white-haired man with a goatee, and the letters KFC.

Col. Harlan Sanders and Kentucky Fried Chicken had made it to Abbottabad.

I had seen the real Col. Sanders several times at restaurants in Washington, DC, and Los Angeles. As he walked to his table, other diners called out: "Try the chicken, Colonel."

We entered.

"Do they have any fish?" Elfie asked. "All we've eaten since we arrived is chicken or mutton."

"I'm not sure KFC's, even in America, offer fish," I said. "Just fried chicken. Kentucky style."

We ordered chicken cooked by the original recipe, French fries and Coca-Colas. A real American fast food meal. The Colonel, I thought, would have been pleased.

Before we got back in the SUV, Elfie and I went for a walk to stretch our legs. We felt safe because of the schools and the army garrison and military academy. It was the Pakistan I remembered from my first visits where anyone could walk anywhere freely.

We continued north. Each town we passed was swarming with people. In one village, the road was barely wide enough for two vehicles to pass, and when two cars approached each other, pedestrians almost had to stand atop shopkeepers' merchandise on the sidewalk.

The road kept climbing. We entered the area ravaged by a 7.6 earthquake on the morning of October 8, 2005. More than 18, 000 people were killed. More than 42, 000 were injured. Tremors were felt as far away as Kabul to the west and New Delhi to the east.

"Could we see what has been done to rebuild?" I asked.

Shabir turned off the KKH. Signs declared that we were in an earthquake reconstruction zone. Most of the reconstruction seemed to have been finished. Few people were on the road. If anyone was still living in a tent it was well out of sight.

"Are these the new houses?" I asked. The houses were gray plastered stone, one story cubes with few windows, and scattered like leaves after a windstorm.

"Yes," Shabir replied.

"Disappointing," I said. "I had hoped that the builders would use new concepts of city planning to site the houses and would have used solar panels or even double-shell solar design to keep the house warm in winter and cool in summer without outside power or wood."

"They probably didn't have the money," Elfie said as we returned to the KKH.

30

Besham lies along the Indus River, midway between Rawalpindi and Gilgit. It is a popular overnight stop for people traveling north or south. Just south of the town, Shabir turned the car down a steep hill. We passed a group of newly-constructed three storey buildings.

"What are those?" I asked.

"Dormitories for Chinese workers," Shabir answered. "They're building a hydroelectric power station a short way down the river."

Two men standing by the road stared at us. They were wearing black turbans.

"Those are Taliban," Shabir said.

Elfie pulled her scarf tighter around her head. I looked at them and wondered if they, like the officials we had met in Peshawar, were tracking our movements.

Shabir stopped the car in the courtyard in front of a beige concrete building. A sign said "PTDC Motel." The manager was waiting by the door. He led us to a room overlooking the Indus.

The room was dark and bare. The bathroom contained a bucket for washing.

"That's all we have," the manager said.

Elfie grinned. "It's OK," she said.

It was a beautiful setting. A few feet from our door was a green lawn and, on a low embankment, a large gray satellite dish. The embankment sloped gently down to the river, which flowed over rocks, churning up whitecaps. In the distance were tall mountains. The only distraction was muffled explosions from the Chinese construction site less than a mile down the Indus.

The Indus River system is one of the world's largest and most important. The Indus begins as a thin stream at one of the sacred mountains of Buddhism, Mt. Kailas, a 22, 000 foot peak in central Tibet. It runs for nearly 2, 000 miles through Tibet, India and Pakistan. Seven major tributaries feed it: on the west, the Kabul and Kurram Rivers; on the east, the five rivers of Punjab: the Jhelum, Chenab, Ravi, Beas and Sutlej. The Indus drains an area almost equal to the combined area of France, Italy and Germany. Its name comes from the Sanskrit word for river, "sindu", and it gave its name to India. It irrigates most of Pakistan.

We had tea on the lawn with Berham and Shabir. The sun had set and the night was getting cold. Shabir finished his tea and left. He came back a few minutes later.

"Musharraf has just declared a state of emergency," he said. A State of Emergency in Pakistan is just short of martial law, which allows the Army to take complete charge.

I wasn't concerned. Pakistan seemed to fall into a governmental crisis or "state of emergency" every time I had been there.

We went into the restaurant. The staff were huddled in front of a small TV in the lounge area. The only other guests were three women wrapped in long scarves. They were speaking English with a flat mid-Western accent.

"Where are you from? I asked.

"Colorado," one said. "We're going up to Kashgar in China."

"Good," I said. "I've been there three times. It's an interesting place. Be sure and go to the Sunday market."

I joined Efie and Shabir at a table near the TV set. The TV pictures showed grim faced soldiers sitting in trucks or standing at barricades in Islamabad. The news was in Urdu. Periodically, an anchor team, a man and a woman, interrupted. They spoke in English.

"Is this a state of emergency under the PCO [Provisional Constitutional Order]" the anchor woman asked.

"It's not clear," the man replied. "Benezir Bhutto says it must be martial law because it was done by the military." Their conversation continued in Urdu.

"Is there an English language channel?" I asked Berham.

"Only Pakistani," he said. "The international channels have been blocked. We can't get CNN, BBC, or Geo."

Shabir picked up his cell phone. It had no dial tone. It, too, had been blocked.

The TV commentators made an announcement in English. Musharraf would appear on television late in the evening to explain why he had declared a State of Emergency and what it meant.

We ate dinner hoping for more news. The commentators kept speculating on what the State of Emergency meant and what Musharraf would say.

We didn't wait for Musharraf's speech. We went to our room. The gentle rush of the Indus outside our room lulled us to sleep. I wondered what conditions were like in Islamabad. I thought back to Kamran Shafi's remark at the Islamabad Club. Something had been done.

The next morning, we entered Kohistan, one of the most isolated and deprived districts in the entire Northwest Frontier Province (NWFP). The name means "land of mountains". The British called it Yaghistan, land of the ungovernable. Even today, the Pakistan government exercises little control. Only about two percent of the people can read or write. They earn a living from livestock. In the winter, the men go to the cities in search of work. Travelers are advised not to wander far from the KKH.

"If we stop," Berham told us, "stay in the car."

A few miles down the KKH, Elfie raised her camera to take a picture of a group of villagers. Berham instantly pushed it down, out of sight.

"This is the only place in Pakistan where I have been at all worried about my safety," I told Elfie. "It was on the trip with Mr. Nazir."

"Who is Mr. Nazir?" Elfie asked.

"He was my guide for part of a trip to Pakistan in 1990," I said.

31

I remembered that trip well. I had wanted to travel with a backpack and no schedule. I wanted to explore the country on my own, staying as long as I wanted wherever I found something interesting, talking with people informally.

That changed when I went to the Pakistan Embassy in Washington to get a visa. The Embassy's astute press secretary, Malik Zahor Ahmed, noticed that I had written "writer" as my occupation on the visa application form. He called me in.

"We can't let you travel alone," he said. "Some areas of Pakistan are still dangerous. Let us make arrangements for you. We can suggest a guide and driver. You will be a VVIP, a Very Very Important Person."

I knew what the grade inflation from VIP meant. I would have a handler.

"I don't want that," I said.

"It will be better," he answered. "You will be treated well."

Reluctantly, I agreed, but I said I would pay all my own expenses. I didn't want to be indebted.

The Pakistan Tourist Development Corporation office in Rawalpindi was to be my contact point and Saeed and Raja

Changez Sultan, then manager of the office and, incidentally, one of Pakistan's most noted artists, had become my friends.

One afternoon, after exploring Rawalpindi on my own, I checked into the PTDC office, as had become my custom.

"We have a guide for you," Saeed said. "He's from our office in Abbottabad. His name is Muhammad Nazir Qureshi, but we call him James Bond because he can get you out of any trouble."

That was not reassuring.

A few minutes later an energetic man strode into the office. He was wearing two-tone red shoes and a rust-red shalwar kameez. His curly black hair was cut long and was touched up with blond highlights.

"This is Mr. Nazir," Saeed said. "I wanted to take you myself, but my boss said he'd have to close the office if I left."

"I'm sorry you can't come," I said. I was deeply disappointed. Saeed would have been fun to travel with. I turned to Mr. Nazir.

"I'm sure I'm in good hands," I said.

The next morning, Mr. Nazir introduced our driver. He was a stocky man with a ready smile. His name was Inyatullah Khan. I would call him Mr. Inyat, as I would call Nazir, Mr. Nazir, out of respect and courtesy.

"Inyat prays five times a day," Mr. Nazir told me as we walked to the two-door Pajero jeep, which would be our transportation.

On that trip, we stopped outside a town called Dobair, close to a churning river that fed into the Indus. Nearby was a tea shop in a line of open-fronted shops facing the road. The roof was corrugated iron resting precariously on thick tree branches. The parking lot was filled with trucks loaded with squared off logs. The trucks were painted with brightly-colored pictures and inspirational sayings: "God is Love," "Health and Wealth," "Love Thy Neighbor." The owner of one of the shops had decorated a tree with huge worn-out truck tires, painted white and hung on spikes like donuts.

Travel advice in America used to be: "Eat where truckers eat."

I was hungry and I was pleased when we pulled into the parking lot.

Mr. Inayatt left to wash and pray. Mr. Nazir left me in a windowless room. It had a small table and enough rope charpois to furnish a dormitory. I sat at the table in a wooden chair. A ceiling fan hung motionless above me.

A boy about ten years old came in and offered me a plate of apricots. I tasted one. It was hard and bitter.

"No, thank you," I said, shaking my head.

The boy left. His face was expressionless.

The room was hot and full of flies. The ceiling fan hung motionless. A man wearing dirty shalwar kameez came in. He looked up at the fan and opened a black box on the wall. He changed a fuse. The fan didn't move. He left.

I went outside. The wind had brought rain. Large raindrops fell on the dirt like buckshot. I sat on a charpoi under the shelter of a leafy tree. A man with dirty clothes and missing teeth walked up and sat too closely beside me. He smiled and asked me a question in a language I didn't understand.

"I speak only English," I said.

He looked at me with eyes that did not seem to focus.

I tried a Hindu word. "Mirbani," I said. "Thank you."

The man got up and left. I felt a sense of menace. The buildings and the people were dirty and disheveled. But there was something else, indefinable.

Another man brought me a mug of tea. The mug was filthy. The rim was crusted with sugar and dirt. I drank a sip and wondered how I could throw it all away.

Mr. Nazir returned. "Where is Inyat?" he asked in an anxious voice.

I pointed to the roof of a low building.

"There," I said. Mr. Inyat was on his knees praying.

Mr. Nazir took my arm and pulled me to the car. I sat in the back seat, relieved to be in my own sanctuary.

32

Elfie and I didn't stop. We crossed the Indus at the twin settlements of Komila, a small bazaar on the west bank and Dasu, the Kohistan administrative center.

"Now starts the rough part," I told Elfie. The road began climbing. The pavement was broken. The river gorge narrowed. The Indus was several thousand feet below us. There were no guard rails. The sheer rock face of the mountain rose starkly on our right.

We passed small monuments. They memorialized shaheeds, martyrs, workers who had been killed in constructing the road. "More workers were killed here than in any other part of the construction," I said.

I looked to see if Elfie was scared. She didn't say anything, but she was biting her lip. "It was dangerous then, but it's all right now," I said.

"Not dangerous now? Look," she exclaimed as we passed a road crew pulling up a car that had missed a curve and fallen into the Indus. A minute or so later, we passed over a patch of unpaved road that threw us about in the SUV.

"A trip up the KKH had always been risky," I said. "There were no guard rails. The fragile shale that makes up the mountains frequently slips down to cover the road. Sometimes, the highway is completely obliterated. On one trip, we had to stop while a yellow bulldozer smeared with dirt pushed the rocks aside. The Northern Frontier Corps had stationed men and bulldozers every few miles. The road crews had a sense of humor. When we finally went through, we saw that they had put up a sign saying 'Relax. Out of Slide Area. Have a Good Drive.'

I was not sure my words reassured her.

The highway descended until it was only a few hundred feet above the Indus. A boy in his early teens was standing beside the road holding five fish tied to a string.

"There's your fish," Berham said.

"Shabir, stop!" I said.

The boy came to the window.

"How much?" Berham asked.

"Five rupees."

I handed Barham a five rupee note.

The boy handed the fish to Elfie. She held the string with the fish in front of her and began laughing.

"What now?" she asked.

"We can have them for lunch," I answered. "They should be good. There is nothing better than really fresh fish."

Shabir pulled into the driveway in front of the Chilas Inn. His cell phone rang. He handed the phone to me. "It's Saeed," he said.

"What are conditions like in Islamabad under the State of Emergency?" I asked.

"It's quiet," he said. "Better than before."

We walked into the lobby of the inn. Shabir handed the fish to the manager.

"Just grill them," I said.

I turned to Elfie. "Grilling is best. Once," I explained, "I had been longing for fish and when it came it was so smothered with curry sauce that I couldn't taste anything but the sauce."

The manager's assistant led Elfie to a hotel room so that she could freshen up. "That's so very thoughtful," she told me when she returned.

We ate in the garden. The fish were bony. They tasted of river mud. We washed them down with cups of hot tea and French-fried potatoes.

The inn's owner sat down beside me.

"The government is going to build a dam here," he said. "It's necessary because Pakistan needs water, but the dam will flood us out. What should we do?"

"Rebuild on the lake front," I suggested. "It will make the inn even more attractive. It will be a resort. You'll get more tourists."

"That's what I thought," he said. "I just wanted to see if you agreed."

We left a few minutes later. A few miles to the north we approached a newly-constructed suspension bridge across the Indus. It was wide enough for only one car, and it was guarded by two men holding rifles. It led to a newly-paved asphalt road, which glistened like polished ebony in the afternoon sun. The road climbed a hillside, turned through a mountain defile and disappeared deep in the sandy, parched mountains.

"The road goes to a Taliban camp," Shabir said.

"Shabir likes Mullah Omar," Berham said, smiling, referring to the violently anti-American leader of the Taliban.

Shabir shook his head in disagreement. "No," he said emphatically. "No!"

Later, Shabir gave me a Taliban propaganda film on a DVD. It opened with a Taliban leader, wearing a long dark green coat with a hood, standing before several dozen young men, who were seated on the ground, wearing white headbands and black scarves and holding rifles pointed toward the sky. Behind the leader stood two prisoners dressed in khaki shalwar kameez. Their faces were covered with black scarves. Their hands were tied behind their backs.

The DVD ended with two young boys, barely on the verge of adolescence, cutting off the head of a uniformed captive. The captive was lying on his side. The boys used a long-bladed knife. It had a dull edge. The beheading took several minutes. The boys used the knife in a sawing motion until they got to the spinal column, which they cut with chopping blows. When the head was severed they held it up, as a trophy, and then put it on the blood-soaked body. The eyes were still open.

An hour or so after we passed the road to the Taliban camp, a dark blue Northwest Frontier Corps bus passed us heading south. Another followed. And another. And another.

"They are going to the Taliban training camp," Shabir said. "They will want revenge for the Taliban killing three policemen last week."

33

A thin white barrier pole on a pivot blocked the highway. Shabir stopped. Three policemen walked toward the car. Berham got out. He followed the policemen toward a low stone building. They stopped at a long table. He showed his identification to another policeman, who opened a log book. Berham signed it.

"This is pretty standard," I told Elfie. "A lot of travelers don't like it. On previous trips, I noticed that many people used phony names. People have signed in as Prince Charles, or Charlemagne, or Mick Jagger. But people have been lost in these areas, and it does help to have an accurate record."

The policemen raised the barrier pole and waved us through. I assumed Berham had signed our real names.

A few hours later, Elfie leaned over the front seat. "I have to go to the toilet," she said. "I had a lot of tea at Chilas."

The road was desolate. There were no gas stations or other facilities.

"Can you wait about fifteen minutes?" Berham asked. "We should get to Gilgit soon."

Forty minutes later, Elfie said. "I really have to go."

We had come to a wide area of the highway. "We could stop here," Berham said. "We'll hide you from the road."

"Yeah, sure," Elfie said, smiling. "I've seen the buses that use the KKH. The seats in the buses are too high for you to hide me."

Shabir pulled the car off the road. Sheer mountain walls loomed on our left. Large gray boulders littered the open space. A stone observation platform overlooked the mountains on our right.

Elfie walked behind the platform. The ground dropped off to the Indus several hundred feet below. I stood in front of her, making a screen with her shawl. Berham and Shabir stood by the road trying to block the view from passing cars, buses, and trucks.

Elfie stood up again, and we walked to the observation platform. Shabir had said we should look at it. A map and a sign painted on stone marked it as more than just an observation post. "The junction point of the three mightiest mountain ranges of the world," it read. The map showed the Himalayan, Karakoram, and Hindu Kush mountains meeting.

"You chose a geologically significant spot," I told Elfie.

"Of course," she replied, nonchalantly, tossing her shawl over her shoulder, "nothing less would do."

A few miles farther on, the road descended. It became smooth and wider. The arid mountains gave way to planar trees and houses set in lush gardens. We passed a one storey modern building with plate glass windows. Signs advertised a business center, FAX machines, e-mail, and even a small mosque. Stately gasoline pumps stood near the highway. They were far different from the gas stations I remembered: small buildings where you used a rotary hand pump to pump your own gas from metal barrels.

We passed pedestrians and sheep and goats and horses. Soon sidewalks flanked the roadway and we entered heavy traffic. We were in Gilgit.

Gilgit lies in a wide valley 4, 000 feet above sea level, midway between Islamabad and the Chinese border. It is a green oasis fed by carefully laid out irrigation canals.

Gilgit began as a market town. Later, it became an administrative center. After partition of India and Pakistan, it grew as a major military staging post, important if India and Pakistan went to war over Kashmir.

We passed a small helicopter, painted olive drab and displayed on a concrete pedestal behind a high iron fence. White lettering said "Indian Army."

"That was captured by Saeed's uncle, Major Hamid," Shabir said. "It crashed in a battle near here, and he captured it for Pakistan."

I wanted to take a picture of it. Shabir stopped the car, but a soldier standing sentry duty nearby motioned for us to move on. I took a picture through the car window.

We continued on to the Serena Lodge, one of a chain of elegant hotels owned by the Aga Khan, spiritual leader of Ismaili Muslims. Uniformed guards stood at the entrance gate. Shabir drove slowly past them and stopped the car in the cobblestone courtyard at the front entrance.

I could sense Elfie's delight as we walked up the steps. After two days of rough travel and a night in a sparse hotel, we were entering first class accommodations.

"I've stayed in a few Serena Lodges before," she told me. "My favorite is Samburu, in Kenya, where I could see elephants bathing in a river."

A bright red and white patterned carpet covered the lobby floor. The walls were brightly varnished wood. Two young men in blue blazers, white shirts, and striped neckties stood behind the reception desk. One of them typed our names into a computer. Seconds later, he gave us the registration form and our room key.

We opened the door. Elfie looked to the left as we walked in.

"A real shower!" she exclaimed. "And real coffee to drink."

Within minutes, she had washed her hair. Then she jumped on the bed with delight.

34

Shah Khan came to the hotel after breakfast. Militarily erect, he was wearing a tailored brown tweed jacket over a tattersall shirt. A brown paisley ascot was tucked neatly into the open collar.

I introduced him to Elfie. We sat in an alcove off the lobby. I handed him a copy of the March 1932 *National Geographic Magazine*, which contained the article "First Over the Roof of the World by Motor." [13] It had photographs of Hunza.

"I thought you might be interested in this," I said.

His face brightened when he came across a picture of a boy dressed in what the photo caption described as "occidental attire," a jacket, vest, white shirt and striped necktie.

"That's my brother," he said with delight.

"I've read *Language Hunting in the Krakoram*, Elizabeth Lorimer's book," Elfie said. "Do you remember Mrs. Lorimer?"

Shah Khan smiled. "Of course," he said, "I was her favorite."

Mrs. Lorimer had described Shah Khan on their first meeting at the Mir's fort as "the loveliest boy of thirteen I have ever seen. He was… one of the Mir's youngest sons, but I christened him forthwith Little Lord Fauntleroy. Short dark curls framed his homespun

---

13   "First Over the Roof of the World by Motor", op. cit

cap, and with him were two playmates armed with wooden rifles, whom he calls his 'bodyguard'." [14]

Shah Khan was an unusually skilled athlete, horseman, hunter, sportsman, mountaineer and, as I had learned when I first met him years before at Saeed's house, a national hero. He was one of the leaders of the attempt to take Muslim Kashmir from India at the time of partition in 1947.

The Pakistanis and Indians are still fighting over Kashmir in the northern part of India. Most historians, relying on Indian histories, say the invasion of Kashmir from the northern areas was started by Pakistan.

That is not true.

In the late Nineteenth Century, the British put the north of India, including Hunza and Nagar and the other small mountain kingdoms, under nominal control of the Maharaja of Kashmir. The lands were so remote and economically insignificant that the maharaja never fully exercised control. Governance remained with the Mirs of Hunza and Nagar.

When the British granted independence to India, the maharaja, a Hindu, dithered as to whether to bring his predominantly Muslim state into India or, as was logical to many people, join Muslim Pakistan. The new Indian government, under Jawaharlal Nehru, pressured him to join India.

He did.

In Gilgit, there was consternation. No one wanted to be under Hindu domination. "We wanted to set up a separate nation," Shah Khan told me. "We were going to call it "The Islamic Republic of the North."

Secret meetings ran late into the night. Out of those meetings grew a plan. The Gilgit Scouts, a lightly-armed and highly-mobile civilian force, would march east through Baltistan and try to take

14   Lorimer, op. Cit, p108

over Kashmir. Shah Khan was one of the leaders. He was then 22. He was the youngest of the group and because, as one historian wrote, he was "stout and stalwart," and the son of the late Mir of Hunza Sir Mohammad Nizam Khan and uncle of the then ruler, Jamal Khan, he was given command of one of the three forces that would march into India.

It was called Eskimo Force. It was made up of about 100 men from Hunza. Its task: hit the Kashmir forces at the strategically important towns of Kargil, Dras and Kharol bridge. Kargil, in the days of caravans, had been a major trading post. It still held vital communications lines. If the Kashmiri forces had been allowed to control it, the whole effort for independence would have failed.

Shah Khan had moved his forces from Gilgit to Chilam, on the Desoi plains south of Gilgit. He had, as he later recalled, "some serious problems of command and control, mutual support, supplies, and much needed decisions on the spot." But as soon as he had orders, he marched to Gultari, the nearest village.

"We had to cross barren mountains, mountains that were perpetually buried in snow," he told me. "There were no roads, not even a path, through Baltistan. It was up and down. Up and down."

The mountain passes reached heights of more than 16, 000 feet. Snow made travel treacherous.

Shah Khan described it more fully in his unpublished memoirs. "Throughout those sixty miles there was no chance of any rest because there were no tents, no sleeping bags and, the worst of all, no dry wood for warming up or cooking food," he wrote. "The moment they [his troops] stopped, they were to be frozen or buried under snow. Safety hung on constant march, day and night, with no fresh food, no medicine, and no rest. It was a feat unexpected of human experience. On April 28th they prepared food for three days because that was the maximum they could carry with them. After three days, they had to depend on their own. Throughout the entire trek even drinking water was not available. The Scouts had to swallow snow in order to quench their thirst."

"Heroic," I said when he first told me the story.

"It was tedious," he replied. "Tedious and boring."

Later, he would tell me: "If we had been older, we would have known that it couldn't be done. But we were young, and we did it."

They also were tough. For centuries, before the British put an end to it, boys in Hunza had been trained to raid caravans. Part of that training was to swim the bitter cold Hunza river in winter and, as one Gilgiti told me, "to jump around on the mountains."

Shah Khan's Scouts reached Gultari on May lst. The local people welcomed them; they did not want to be governed by India. Three days later, the Scouts left Gultari and marched further into Kashmir. At Kunar, they finalized the plan for attack. Shah Khan had divided his troops into three groups. They would disperse and attack the Kargil bridge on May 7th.

The attack was successful. At Kargil, they linked up with another group from Gilgit. It was called the Ibex Force. It had come from Skardu in Baltistan by another route, and while the Eskimos stayed in western Kashmir, the Ibex Force advanced across the top of India.

The Government of India could find no way to stop them. Winter snows blocked troops and heavy weapons. The Indians decided intimidation might work; they would bomb Gilgit. The Indian planes flew low to scare the Gilgitis. The Gilgatis were not frightened. As the planes approached, the Scouts' bag pipe band marched onto the airfield. Inspired by a series of Scottish political officers and commandants, the Gilgitis were immaculately dressed in uniforms of Black Watch tartan. They stood in orderly formation and played marches as the Indian planes flew over.

By the end of June 1948, the Scouts' forces had cleared the Maharaja's troops from most of Kashmir and penetrated far into Kashmir. They surrounded Leh, the capital of the Ladakh district,

11, 500 feet high in the Himalayas and some 100 miles from India's border with China and 200 miles from Gilgit. But warmer weather opened the passes blocked by winter snow. The Government of India sent in troops and armored tanks. The Government of Pakistan, which had initially known nothing of the Scouts' invasion, decided to take over.

On January 1, 1949, Pakistan and India signed a cease fire agreement. The western part of Kashmir went to Pakistan; the eastern part to India. A plebiscite, to which India agreed, would allow the people of Kashmir to decide which nation to join, India or Pakistan. The plebiscite has never been held. The dispute still simmers. Troops are stationed atop the snow-covered mountains on both sides of the border. Skirmishes periodically break out. The area remains a tinder box, made all the more frightening by the fact that India and Pakistan now have nuclear weapons. The possibility of war with India has shadowed Pakistan's foreign and domestic policy for more than sixty years.

35

Shabir invited us to lunch at his mother's house. His brother and two children joined us. Shabir's mother was beautiful and shy. She welcomed us warmly. She lives in a large, rambling gray stone house with blue trim, set on green lawns in the center of Gilgit. Shabir and his brother also lived there. Shabir gave us a tour of the house, which had large, comfortably-furnished rooms.

Berham joined us. We ate on the lawn and spoke of our travels and of our families. Shabir's mother spoke no English, but she and Elfie communicated using pantomime, and touching and laughing. Occasionally, Shabir would translate.

At the end of lunch, Shabir looked at his watch.

"We had better leave for the polo game," he said.

"Gilgit has changed so much," I told Elfie as we drove through the town. "Like everything else in Pakistan. It has more people, more cars, more congestion. I hardly recognize it."

I looked for a small square in the middle of the bazaar, where several roads came together. It was there, years before, that I decided Gilgit was a good place to buy a goat. At least, after Eid.

"Eid-ul-Ajha is the two day festival commemorating the sacrifice of Ismail," I told Elfie. "Muslims believe it was Ismail, not

Issac, whom Abraham offered to sacrifice to God. For days, before Eid started, the small fenced-in square in Gilgit had been full of shaggy goats, full grown and fat, waiting to be bought for sacrifice. Usually, the oldest male in a household slits the goat's throat, and the meat is divided into three parts, one for relatives and neighbors, one for the poor, and one for the household."

"How much did a goat cost?" Elfie asked.

"I was told the prices ranged from 2, 000 to 2, 500 rupees," I answered. "That was about $100 or $125 at the then-current rate of exchange.

"I hope you did not buy one," she said.

"No," I answered. "I was wearing jeans and a white button down shirt and didn't look like I really wanted to buy a goat. I didn't pursue the conversation with the goat seller, but a few days later, after Eid, I noticed that a score of goats were left unsold. 'How much would a goat cost?' I asked another man who was standing inside the square.'Six hundred rupees,' he said.

"It was a post-holiday sale," I told Elfie, "but I still didn't want to buy a goat. I think animal sacrifice is barbaric. I don't think I'm alone. After that Eid, I bought a copy of *The Muslim*, a newspaper published in Islamabad. Several articles criticized the practice of slaughtering a goat for Eid. The paper said that the practice was too expensive for poor people, and it claimed that, in the early days of Islam, Muhammad had slaughtered a goat for everyone and for all time, and that no one need do it now. But it's hard to change customs that go back so far in history."

I remembered something else. "Oh," I added, "on that day, an amusing thing happened. It reflected the sophistication of the Aga Khan's sect of Islam. On my way back through the bazaar, a muzzein was calling prayers from the mosque. I was walking behind two men. One turned to the other. "We Ismailis don't need a call to prayer," he said. "We have watches."

Shabir let us out at Gilgit's Aga Khan Polo Field. A simple sign marked the stadium entrance: "Let other people play at other things – the King of Games is still the Game of Kings."

Once, every village in the Northern Areas had a polo field. Today, the fields still exist, but not every village has its own team. In Gilgit, games are held weekly. Teams are made up of men from military units stationed in Gilgit. I wanted to introduce Elfie to the game, and also had hoped I could see two old friends, Darwesh Ali, one of the stars of the Gilgit team, and Raji Rehmet, the team captain.

"Any chance that we can see Darwesh or Raji?" I asked Shabir.

"Both are dead," he replied. "They had heart attacks right after polo matches."

I was saddened.

We sat in spectators' stands above the field. Eight musicians sat on a concrete platform on the opposite side of the field. We could barely hear them playing. The game was sparsely attended, slow, and, I thought, boring. Then, one of the players grabbed the polo ball in mid-air and, holding it high in his right hand, galloped from center field to his opponents' goal. His team mates formed a barricade on each side to protect him. The spectators, who had been unenthusiastic for most of the match, burst into applause.

The game was won.

"Amazing," I said to Shabir.

"It was Darwesh's son," Shabir replied. "He's playing for the Northern Light Infantry."

Later, Berham brought him to the stands. He was tall and looked like his father.

Elfie, one of only two women watching the game, moved from her seat so that we could talk.

"Congratulations on your goal," I said. "I've never seen anything like it."

He smiled.

"I considered your father a good friend," I continued. "I was saddened to hear of his death. I had looked forward to introducing my wife, Elfie, to him. We have a picture of him practicing at Shandur in our house."

"Thank you," he said.

"The Northern Light Infantry must be a good outfit."

"Yes," he said. "We're soon to be sent to Sudan as part of a UN peace keeping mission."

"I'm sure you'll do well."

He left and Elfie returned to her seat. It was damp with sweat. He had played a hard game.

36

On my first visit to Gilgit in 1988, I asked Riaz Ahmed Khan, the PTDC manager for the Northern Areas, about the history of the area, of Gilgit, Hunza, and Nagar.

"I'm interested in the history and I talk to the old people so that it won't be lost," he told me. "I will teach you. The history has never been written."

We sat on the veranda of the Chinar Inn, outside his office. He looked at me questioningly.

"How old are you?" he asked.

I told him.

"I'm a few years younger. Do you mind that I be your teacher?"

"No," I said. "Age doesn't always mean wisdom. You have knowledge I don't have."

He nodded in agreement.

"Then, we can meet at this time every day," he said.

Riaz was in his early forties. He was tall and thin, with an aquiline nose. His hair was black, graying at the temples and cut long on one side so that it fell over his forehead.

We started the first lesson the next day. He sat opposite me in a room next to the reception desk.

"I don't smoke," he announced before we began, holding up two fingers as though holding a cigarette. "I don't drink tea or watch television."

"Why are you so pure?" I asked, smiling.

"I just never have," he replied.

I turned on my small tape recorder just as a van load of vacationing Pakistanis disgorged into the reception room. The children looked as if they would rather be anywhere else. The women were not veiled. The men wore shorts so brief that I could see part of their buttocks. One man stood with his back toward me and kept scratching his spine, exposing masses of hair under his T-shirt.

The tourists wanted rooms and information. They were loud and arrogant. Riaz got up to help them. I excused myself.

We began again, the next day. "Many groups have ruled The Northern Areas," Riaz said. "Iranians, Aryans, Arabs, Chinese, soldiers of Alexander the Great." He paused while I wrote in a small leather notebook.

"Gilgit," Riaz continued, "was part of the Buddhist kingdom of Bolor from the third to the 11th Century. That is why there are still signs of Buddhism, the rock carvings, for example, including the Kargah Buddah outside of Gilgit. By the 11th Century, the Gilgit area had become a powerful independent kingdom. It was called Dardistan, the land of the ungovernable, and it was as strong as Kashmir.

"Later, when the strong central power declined, each isolated valley became a small kingdom. There were seven kingdoms along the Gilgit and Hunza Rivers alone; five different languages were spoken. The kingdoms were constantly at war. But they were rich, because they taxed or raided caravans that came down along the rivers. It was part of the Silk Route between China and the West."

"When did Islam come in?" I asked.

"Sometime after the 11th Century," he answered. "But I should start with the history of the rulers. There is a legend still told in

Gilgit. It tells the origin of the family that ruled for almost a millennium. That's my family. My great-grandfather was Mir of Hunza."

Here is that story as I told it to Elfie.

"Every nation has a legend about its founding, or its founding heroes," I said. "In America, for example, we hold George Washington up as a model for young people and one of the stories about him is that he never told a lie. When he chopped down his father's cherry tree, he said "yes, I did it.""

"What is the one about Hunza?" she asked.

"It's kind of a nasty story."

"What is it?"

"Well, it starts with three Saracen princes who had come to India about a thousand years ago, looking for kingdoms to rule. They had a rough time until they got to Gilgit. There the people were welcoming. One decided to stay. The other two said they felt the people were sad and they wondered why there were no children playing in the streets. So they left. The one who stayed, I think his name was Abdul Azur Jamshad, learned that people were sad because the Buddhist ruler, called Shri Badat, was a cannibal. He had a fondness for human babies and was such a tyrant that the people could do nothing to him."

"That's horrible."

"Well, the story is that Abdul eventually married Shri Badat's daughter and when she got pregnant they decided they had to find a way to kill her father so that he wouldn't eat their baby. She told her father that she could protect him from angry villagers if he would tell her what his vulnerabilities were."

Here I tried to imitate a tyrant king by making my voice angry. "Swords, arrows, axes cannot kill me," he said. 'I am vulnerable only to fire, for my heart is made of butter."

"Butter?" Elfie interrupted.

"Yeah, I guess butter was precious," I said in my normal voice. "Anyway, the daughter, along with Abdul, and the king's Wazir, or prime minister, decided to trick old Shri Badat. That night, they dug a trench on the polo grounds near his fort, filled it with firewood, and erected a tent over it. Then, they told him that the villagers were having a festival and he went down and sat in a specially-built throne to watch. Bam! As soon as he was seated they cut the ropes of the tent and lit the firewood."

"And that was the end of the king?"

"Not quite. He had magic and he appeared in a couple of other places asking for water, but the farmers he asked didn't understand him and gave him liquor. That did kill him off. But up until about fifty years ago people in Gilgit built a bonfire, which they called the 'Tumushelling Bonfire' to insure that he didn't come back. The place is at the end of the airfield landing strip. It's now a park."

"What does that have to do with Hunza."

"I was coming to that. When Abdul became king, the kingdom prospered. But the people north of Gilgit, the people in Hunza and Nagar, complained that they were paying taxes but were getting nothing back. No money for troops or defense. So Abdul sent his two sons north to rule. One, called Girkis, which means mouse, got Hunza. The other one, called Muglot, a word for a male mongoose, got Nagar."

"And everyone lived happily ever after?"

"Not quite. Hunza was considered the better of the two districts. And Muglot plotted to get it. He invited his brother to dinner and poisoned him. The people of Hunza were not too happy with this. They went to war. They fought for centuries, even though the ruling families intermarried. The British finally put a stop to it."

"Is the story about the cannibal king true?"

"I don't know. Some researchers say it reminded them of similar legends in other parts of Asia. But people still tell it and there was the centuries-old custom of the bonfire. So people may have believed it or just liked the custom, a sort of shared experience. Anyway, that's the legend of the founding of the royal line in Hunza and Nagar. It started with a Saracen prince."

37

The mountain kingdoms followed the practice of royal families in other parts of the world. One ruler of Hunza married a princess from Skardu, which had been the western edge of the Tibetan empire. She brought 500 workers who built her a new house, Altit Fort, which sits flush with a sheer cliff one thousand feet above the Hunza River. Eight years later, she built another palace, Baltit Fort, high in the hills and well back from the river. Baltit became the principal residence of the Hunza rulers. It is now a museum. Descendents of the workers who built both forts still live in the village of Altit.

Historically, Hunza, Nagar and the rest of what became the Northern Areas was fearsome territory. The Maharaja of Kashmir tried to conquer the area and tribesmen captured his soldiers. Some were used as human fireworks. Others were sold into slavery, as were caravaners who worked their way down the narrow paths along the river. The caravaners had three choices: pay tribute, be sold into slavery, or die.

"In the absence of coin," John Keay writes in "*The Gilgit Game*," mankind was a common currency; a hunting dog cost one male slave and a sturdy pony two females, preferably fair and fourteen."[15]

The area's wild reputation did not deter the British. Occasionally, one or two would venture into the kingdoms. The first who left a notable record was Gustav W. Leitner. He was an ethnologist, linguist, explorer. At age 15, he had been commissioned a colonel in the British Army. At age 25, he was named head of Lahore University. Leitner used his summer vacation to venture alone along the Indus.

Leitner's interest was scientific. Those who followed had political goals: the fear that Russia, seeking to create an empire in Central Asia and gain access to a warm water port in India, would thrust through the mountains. Keeping the Russians at bay became what the sports-loving British called "The Great Game."

To keep an eye on the Russians, the British set up a small "agency" in Gilgit. Totally isolated by snow for eight months of the year, this first outpost was small and remote. In 1881, it was overrun by Kohistani troops, coming up from the south.

In 1889, after the road from Srinigar was improved and a telegraph line built, the British tried again. This attempt was successful. The British brought law and order. They ended the warfare between Hunza and Nagar, but they had to deal with a ruler of Hunza named Safdar Ali.

The story of how Safdar Ali became Mir, as the British dubbed the rulers, is told in the unpublished memoirs of his half-brother Mohomed Nazim Khan, the father of Shah Khan.

I was ill at the time and confined to the Mahal where my father often visited me. One warm day, after meeting with me for some time, he went out for a stroll in the Shumal Bagh where Tara Beg and some of his men were lying concealed. As soon as he appeared they shot him down. Hearing the noise of the firing, I thought at first that a son

15   John Keay, The Gilgit Game, Explorers of the Western Himalayas 1865-95, Karachi, 1990, Oxford University Press; p15

had been born to some influential man in the village, but the sound of rushing feet and the shouting soon convinced me of what had really taken place and seizing a gun, I rushed out of my sickroom, calling to the door-keeper to close the door. But my weakness was so great that I fell unconscious on the threshold where I was found by Safdar Ali and imprisoned for two months.

People rapidly collected and removed the corpse, which was still lying in the Shumal Bagh, and gave it a public burial, after which they intended to put Safdar Ali to death; but he declared a remission of twelve taxes, that had hitherto been a sore burden on the people, and by this means escaped the fate in store for him and secured the country for himself...

The original plan had been that Safdar Ali should murder all his brothers. [This had been the custom to prevent fratricidal warfare. He killed five, throwing two over a precipice. He also killed his own mother.]

I was detained for two months and was then summoned before Safdar Ali. Who looked on me with anger and hatred. He conducted me on foot to my father's tomb where he made me swear, and my following with me, that there would be no intrigue against him. When this was over, he presented me with a choga that Colonel Lockhart had given him, a khatli pony, and a rifle and accouterments; and from that day looked upon me with increasing favor.[16]

The British had their share of kings who resolved succession problems with the chopping block. They didn't look kindly on regicide and parricide, but they put up with Safdar Ali for five years.

Lt. Francis Younghusband, one of the most legendary of all the legendary men who played key roles in The Great Game, disliked Safdar Ali almost immediately. Younghusband had met Safdar Ali in Guilmet, a village in the north of Hunza. Safdar was full of self-importance. "He was under the impression," Younghusband later wrote, "that the

---

16 Sir Mohomed Nazim Khan, KCIE, Mir of Hunza; Unpublished manuscript in author's possession; p 15.

Empress of India, the Czar of Russia, and the Emperor of China were chiefs of neighboring tribes."[17]

Younghusband decided to give a demonstration of British strength. He ordered his Gurka troops to fire at a rock 700 yards across the valley. The Gurkas' six bullets struck the rock simultaneously, and close together.

Safdar was delighted. To him, it was a new game. He spotted a man descending the cliff path opposite and asked Younghusband to order his men to fire at him. Younghusband laughed but explained that they could not do this because they would almost certainly hit the man.

"What does it matter if they do," Safdar said. "After all, he belongs to me."

As Peter Hopkirk notes in *The Great Game*, "This merely confirmed the highly unfavorable opinion of Safdar Ali that Younghusband had acquired during their discussions."[18]

"I knew that he was a cur at heart," Younghusband wrote, "and unworthy of ruling so fine a race as the people of Hunza."

Safdar Ali also antagonized the British by encouraging Russian expectations that they could advance into Hunza, even while he was accepting money from the British to keep them out.

When the British took over Nagar after a hard battle, he knew his time was up and fled to Xingjiang in westernmost China. The British replaced him with Mohamed Nazim Khan, his half brother.

As Elizabeth Lorimer writes, Nazim "had an unusually wide political education. As a boy of only nine or ten he had been sent down by his father as a hostage to Gilgit, and had there met British officers for the first time and gained many new ideas. Later he acted as ambassador and negotiator for his father and brother on missions

---

17 Quoted in Peter Hopkirk, The Great Game, 1990, New York, Kodansdha America, Inc., p 450-61
18 Hopkirk, op. cit., p459-61.

to Chinese Turkestan and Afghanistan, and he could talk Wahi, Turki, Khowar, and Hindustani, as well as his own Burushaski. Above all, he was an extremely able youth, and had drawn his own deductions from his varied adventures."[19]

He was considered a natural diplomat. He had even won the admiration of the Russian Colonel, Bronislav Gramchuski, who had been trying to increase Russian influence in the north of India.

"After [Col. Gramchuski] took his departure," Nazim wrote in his autobiography, "I accompanied him to Altit Fort where I plied him with wine that I might get to learn what he really thought, and he told me that he considered all the rest of them fools and that I was the only one with any real intelligence."

Nazim reigned as Mir from September 1892 until his death forty-six years later. His reign was marked by peace and prosperity. In 1938, shortly before he died, the British awarded him the order of Knight Commander of the Indian Empire.

19   Lorimer, op cit., p121

38

After the polo match, Elfie and I were treated to yet another display of Pakistani hospitality. Berham invited us to dinner with his family. Many courses were served, and Elfie and I were impressed with the quality, quantity, and variety of the food.

"They are so creative in what must be a limited kitchen," she told me after we left. "It's so impressive."

The next morning, we left for Chalt, a small village set back from the KKH, as the road heads higher into the mountains north toward China. Chalt is a collision zone: the tectonic plate that carries the Indian subcontinent and the plate that carries Europe collided there millions of years ago and formed the Himalayan Mountains. The mountains are still rising. A plaque on a sheer rock above the KKH marks the spot. It reads simply:"Where Continents Collided."

In Chalt, we wanted to see a new house Saeed was building.

Saeed had grown up in Chalt. His new house sat in a large field. A cow grazed at one end, beside a stone wall. A large satellite dish rested on the ground near the entrance. We entered from the veranda, which wrapped around two sides of the house. I stopped by the front door and looked back at the mountains.

"Put a couple of rocking chairs here, and you could watch Rakaposhi all day," I said. The mountain looked as majestic and inviting as it must have been to Elizabeth Lorimer, who called it the loveliest mountain on earth.

We walked through the nearly completed house and went back outside. Elfie was excited by the view. She pulled out her sketchbook. She began drawing. She spent half an hour sketching Rakaposhi from different viewpoints.

Chalt is one of the villages of the former kingdom of Nagar. It was our first stop in Nagar. I had a fond memory of Nagar because of one man.

In Islamabad, on a previous trip, Saeed had made an appointment for me to see Mir Shaukat Ali Khan, the former ruler of Nagar. He lived in an unpretentious, modern two-storey house set back from a quiet street. A bright blue jeep, with a blue metal top, was parked under a breezeway. The license plate read "Nagar 1."

I rang the bell and a stocky man with a prominent nose let me in. He was wearing a tan shalwar kameez. On the little finger of his left hand was a silver and agate ring. I introduced myself, and he led me into the living room, furnished in understated elegance. The couches and chairs were upholstered in English chintz. Silent electric fans in the ceiling kept the room cool. A hand-woven Pakistani carpet covered the floor. A large, pea green ceramic horse's head sat on a side table.

The Mir sat on a couch. I sat on an upholstered chair at his side.

"Tea?" he asked. He poured two cups from a ceramic pot resting on a tray on the highly-polished coffee table. He handed me a plate with pound cake and samosas.

"I ruled for 32 years," he said. "Until 1972, when the government of Pakistan abolished hereditary offices. My family descended from the last Saracen kings of Persia. They came to Gilgit and then up to Nagar and Hunza more than 1, 000 years ago.

"We used to trade with the Chinese. We'd exchange gold for whatever we needed."

Herodotus had written that the area was rich in gold dust created by a species of "huge ants, smaller than dogs but larger than foxes." [In 1996, explorers in Northern Pakistan discovered that marmots, not ants, throw up piles of gold-rich earth as they burrow.]

"Now," the Mir continued, "I spend the winters in Islamabad and the summers in Nagar. People still come to see me. They want me to settle disputes, and I do that."

"Do you regret no longer being ruler?" I asked.

"No," he said. "No. Now I am free."

Later, I thanked Saeed for setting up the meeting.

"The Mir is my father-in-law," he said. Saeed's maternal grandfather was Mir of Hunza.

"Is there gold in Nagar, now?" I asked.

"Some," Saeed said. "My father-in-law uses gold to pay for everything. He doesn't believe in paper money." He paused and smiled. "We, his family, wonder where he keeps it. It's probably in the house, but he won't tell anyone where. If he dies, it might be lost."[20]

---

20 Mir Shaukat died in the Spring of 2003. The only gold found was a small bar, probably used for day-to-day expenses at the Islamabad residence. No one knows what happened to the gold at the Nagar palace, if there was any.

39

A few miles after we left Chalt, Shabir turned the SUV off the highway onto a narrow dirt road. We drove for about three miles through a small village until we reached The Diran Hotel.

The lobby of the Diran Hotel had no pictures of Mir Shaukat. I was, however, attracted to a picture of a distinguished man dressed in a long black tailored jacket and a white hat. Around his neck he wore a white ribbon from which was suspended a medal in the shape of an eight-pointed star.

"That's Shabir's grandfather," Israr Hussain, the hotel's manager and stepbrother of the owner, told me. "He was the first president of the Northern Areas after Pakistan became independent."

In another room, there was a picture of the current Mir of Hunza and President George W. Bush shaking hands. "Many tourists do not understand why we have the picture," Israr said. "We tell them that we like George Bush. If he hadn't done something, the Taliban would be here. This is a strategic area. It's the route between China and Afghanistan. The people in Xinjiang, China, are Muslims. They don't like the Chinese. They like the Taliban."

We passed through the lobby. The only other guests were a man and a woman in their twenties, wearing trekking shoes, sitting on a couch intently discussing a map. Their accents were Australian.

We went to the garden. A warm sun was shining in the cloudless sky. The mountains were vivid. Bed sheets were drying on clotheslines. A goat was nibbling grass. "What can we prepare for your meal?" Israr asked.

Elfie pointed to the chickens.

"How about an omelet?" she said.

Israr left to go to the kitchen.

Israr's wife invited Elfie to talk with her and her daughter in the rear of the garden. They lived behind the hotel in an inviting house surrounded by fruit trees.

Elfie talked with them for quite a while.

Walking back, Elfie stopped at a tree filled with ripe red apples.

"Oh," she said to Israr, who had joined her, "may I please have one?"

He picked an apple from a branch and handed it to her.

She took a bite. "Delicious," she said. She ate the whole apple while standing there.

Israr picked some apples and put them into a bag with walnuts and apricots, sun dried on rooftops. He gave the bag to Elfie.

We sat beside a low white metal table a few feet from a side entrance to the hotel. A young man brought out cups of tea.

"It's rose tea, from our garden," Israr said.

"Do you have more children?" Elfie asked Israr.

"Yes," he said. "I want to send them to Islamabad for school, if I have the money. We don't have good schools here. I don't want the Taliban to educate them. The Taliban want to wage a Holy War against America. They tell students that America has taken our things, like our oil. Children don't know. They don't understand."

The young man returned with plates heaped high with dried apricots and walnuts. He came back a few minutes later with French-fried potatoes and an omelet.

Elfie took a forkful of the omelet and smiled. "This is better than La Mere Poulard's famous omelet, which I once ate at Mont San Michel," she said, "the most famous omelet in France, and maybe the world. Or so they claim. For sure, it's the most expensive."

I ate some of the potatoes.

"Are these Nagar potatoes?" I asked Shabir.

Berham and Shabir had been kidding each other for most of the trip about the difference between potatoes grown in Nagar and potatoes grown in Hunza. Each claimed one was better than the other.

"Nagar," Shabir said.

"Hunza," Berham said, with a smile.

I thought back to the start of commercial potato farming in the Northern Areas.

Years ago, an agricultural official from an international development agency wanted to introduce potatoes to Nagar and Hunza as a cash crop and to feed local people. He made one mistake. He began to plant a test plot in a village polo field. He was spotted by Waltraud Torossian-Brigasky, an Austrian who had fallen in love with the Northern Areas and their customs, especially polo, and who was such a frequent visitor that she kept a jeep there.

"You can't dig in that field," she told the official. "Dig somewhere else. That's the village polo field."

"Polo?" he asked. "Here?"

"Yes," she replied. "It is the game of every village. Have some respect for their customs."

Abashed, he took his shovel and bag of potatoes to a wheat field.

Now, a steady commerce of trucks heads south with sacks of potatoes. The seed potatoes came from Holland. They have produced a profitable cash crop. And they are not planted in polo fields.

40

It was dusk when we reached the contiguous villages that make up Hunza. I looked for familiar sites. Hardly anything was as I remembered it. There was little open space; the villages had grown together. The field next to the PTDC hotel where I had stayed, where women were threshing wheat in a field outside my window was now full of shops. Little, if anything resembled the idyllic land Elizabeth Lorimer had romanticized.

Shabir turned up a steep hill toward Karimabad, Hunza's capital. We turned again onto a broad parking lot carved into the hillside. We entered the Hotel Hunza Embassy, a sister to the guest house in Islamabad. We were the only guests; it was past the tourist season.

We had dinner in the empty hotel dining room and went to bed, shivering in the bitter November cold, and clung to each other for warmth.

The next morning, we met the manager.

"Was everything satisfactory?" he asked.

"Yes," I replied. "But it was very, very cold. Uncomfortably cold."

He looked puzzled. "Why did you not turn the heat on?" he asked. "Each room has its own control. You would have been comfortable."

"We didn't see the control," I said. "Next time, we'll know."

Shabir met us. "I'll take you to the foot of Baltit Fort," he said.

Elfie was enchanted by the flat rooftops, where tomatoes, nuts, and laundry were drying in the sunlight. The houses were adorned with intricately carved doors. The view of the mountains, especially Rakaposhi, was breathtaking; the whole area was in its autumn splendor. The women were shy, instantly turning their back or disappearing into doorways. We climbed up another steep hill to Baltit Fort, the former palace of the Mir of Hunza. The stolid building, vaguely Tibetan in appearance, watches over the valley like a sentry. We got out to walk the rest of the way. Children with book bags on their backs walked with us on the stone-paved street. A boy and a girl looked at us over a high stone wall and I stopped to take their picture. The fort was built at the end of the 16th century. The ruling family lived there until 1960, when the reigning Mir built a sprawling gray stone house about a mile away. Baltit Fort became a museum restored with funds from the Historic Cities Support Programme of the Aga Khan Trust for Culture.

I had long wanted to see the inside, but on previous visits, it had been closed for renovation.

With Elfie, I made it only as far as the gift shop. I was suffering from lack of sleep and was not accustomed to the nearly 9, 000 feet altitude. I stumbled into the nearby gift shop and rested in a chair.

Shabir brought the car up the pathway and we left. I was disappointed.

We passed the F.G. Girls College. I noticed a sign. It read "Evolution of Development in Hunza and Nagar." It was a conference sponsored by the Aga Khan Foundation. We stopped and looked into the auditorium. A large screen dominated the front of the room. A power point projector sat on a table facing it. Rows of chairs faced the screen.

People were still registering. We went outside. A man in a beige sport jacket greeted Elfie. "I saw you at the Serena Lodge," he explained.

"What is the Aga Khan Foundation?" she asked after reading his name tag.

"We work for economic development," he said. "There is much still to be done. I travel to small villages. People live like animals. They have no heat, no running water, no indoor plumbing. Conditions are ripe for the spread of disease."

I was surprised that the Aga Khan Foundation still had villages to reach. I had looked into it on a previous visit.

"On my first trip to Hunza," I told Elfie, "it seemed like every village had a small green and white sign posted beside an irrigation canal or bridge or other small development project. The sign always started with the letters AKRSP.

"What is AKRSP?" I had asked.

"It's the Aga Khan Rural Support Program," I was told.

The Aga Khan is head of the world's 15 million Ismaili Muslims. The Ismailis, scattered throughout Asia, Africa, Europe, and North America, are a small number compared with the billion or so Muslims world-wide. They see Islam through modern eyes. Islam, they believe, is a faith that emphasizes intellectual freedom, compassion, tolerance and human dignity.

The Aga Khan Foundation began working to improve conditions in the Northern Areas in 1982. Before the opening of the Karakoram Highway four years later, villagers in Pakistan's northern areas survived on subsistence farming. The late winter months, before bringing in the first crop, were a time of virtual starvation. The AKRSP was to be something new: a laboratory for economic micro-development, education, housing, health, and cultural awareness. The core belief, as stated by the Aga Khan, was "trust in people." He said in a video summation of the Foundation's work, that "an extraordinary phenomenon in development is people changing their own environment."

To start the AKRSP in the Northern Areas, Aga Khan Foundation president Robert Shaw brought in Shoaib Sultan Khan.

In 1993, I had dinner with Shoaib in his apartment at the back of the Chinar Inn. One of his daughters, who had just graduated from the London School of Economics, sat with us. Shoaib was a soft-spoken man. He radiated compassion and intelligence.

"Forty percent of the world's people live below the poverty line," he told me. "The developed world is very much interested in improving the lot of the world's poor, but much of the early euphoria is gone; earlier attempts were not an instant panacea. Fire brigade attempts are not the answer. The AKRSP attempts to build long term solutions. We set up the AKRSP along the lines taught me by Akhter Hameed Khan, who was my mentor and greatest psychological supporter. He believed that democratic village institutions can empower the rural poor. I had started as a civil servant. I was told that I should be responsible for the people in my charge even though I was young and inexperienced. My division had nearly one million people and I was responsible for administering welfare, maintaining law and order, and adjudicating disputes. Our approach was paternalistic: 'We tell the villagers what they should have.'"

By 1972, Shoaib was chief executive of the Metropole District of Karachi. It was a powerful job. He was not satisfied. He asked to be transferred to the Pakistan Academy for Rural Development in Peshawar.

"At first, the Pathans in Peshawar were totally aghast that someone was trying to help them," he told me. "We did not work together. We had to carry firearms."

One day, a colleague said, "God did not send you into the world with a musket."

He changed his approach. Within a year, he and the villagers were meeting to discuss development.

A few years later, he was working in a forest village in Sri Lanka, helping devise a social program for rural settlers under the auspices of UNICEF.

"In December of 1982, Robert Shaw asked me to come back to Pakistan to introduce programs that would generate income for the people in the Northern Areas," he told me. "It was an area of more than a million people, isolated from the rest of the world on more than 72, 000 square kilometers (about 43, 000 square miles). It was a chance to build an infrastructure that would support development. Without institution building, you cannot have micro-development."

He set up an office in one room of an old building in the bazaar in Gilgit. Four days later he met with villagers during a snowstorm in Japauka, a small, isolated village on the road to Chitral. Suspicious of the AKRSP, they were at first reluctant to meet. He convinced them that the AKRSP would help them, and they agreed to build a bridge, providing not only the labor but land and a link to the road. The AKRSP provided engineers and money for materials.

"Our basic philosophy," Shoaib said, "was that physical infrastructure projects provide the best catalysts for collective decision making and accountability in poor rural communities. We then began talking with villagers, explaining our goals. We would give each village a one-time only grant for such a project. But we laid down certain conditions. The villages had to choose the project collectively, and it would have to benefit everyone. They also would have to form an organization to plan, build and maintain the project. They would have to meet regularly with everyone present, and they had to make systematic contributions to a common fund so that there would be savings and collateral to meet future needs. At first there was some skepticism. The villagers said they were too poor to make any contributions. Or they felt that we would try to convert them to the Ishmaili sect.

"But enough agreed and we started with irrigation projects, which were badly needed because much of the land had been worked out. We at the AKRSP monitored what was being done, the new irrigation channels and the link roads. We funneled equipment, supplies, and essential expertise to the village builders."

He paused reflectively. "Some of them were smarter than we were. In one town near the Chinese border, our experts said a link canal couldn't be built because it had to tunnel through rock. The villagers, using their own expertise, built it in a few days.

"When new land was opened for farming, we began urging the villagers onto the next stage. I told them that 'the sooner you develop the land, the sooner you will benefit.' We introduced new strains of plants, taught the villagers new skills, and encouraged the women, the illiterate and ever-toiling women, to assert themselves and set up collective initiatives of their own.

"When we started, we had only a staff of one, me. Now we have about 300 people and we have programs in 1, 400 mountain villages. People there are managing their own livelihood projects, generating income, and conserving local resources. The trees we have supplied, for example, not only anchor the mountain soil, but provide apricots and apples which can be sold "down country," in Pakistan's cities."

41

I asked if I could see one of their projects.

A few days later, Essa Khan, an AKRSP program officer, picked me up at the Chinar Inn. He was about thirty-five years old and he wore a pale blue T-shirt. His tan trousers squeezed his waist. With him was his small son, his uncle, and the driver of the jeep that carried us.

"We'll go to Hamaran Village," he said. "You can see the AKRSP project there."

We drove from Gilgit across a single lane suspension bridge. Once the longest suspension bridge in Asia, it swayed as the car passed over it. We went through several villages and finally onto a narrow dirt road. The road snaked along the mountainside. The jeep had to back up several times to swing around the tight curves. We threaded around giant boulders. The car suddenly stopped. The left rear tire had been torn by a rock. A few hundred yards ahead, the road itself became little more than a wide pathway.

"This is a government road," Essa Khan said. "They don't maintain it."

We walked on. We passed a woman who turned so that we could not see her face. She was walking with a young man and two donkeys. The donkeys were carrying green sheaves of wheat. Earlier, leaving Gilgit, we had passed two donkeys almost invisible under piles of golden wheat. These donkeys were carrying only enough to fill a two gallon bucket.

The road turned and suddenly I saw a long and bright splash of emerald green on a high bluff across a canyon. A handful of houses nestled among the green fields and trees. A concrete platform with a target circle painted on it rested incongruously at one end of the bluff. It was a landing field for helicopters used by development experts.

"Is that the village?" I asked.

"That is Hamaran Village," Essa Khan said.

The road descended toward the river and turned. On our left, four men were hammering narrow balusters along the sides of a new suspension bridge. It arched over the deep river chasm and glowed of new wood and shining steel cables.

"This is a villagers' project," Essa Khan said, adding proudly, "with help from the AKRSP."

We walked gingerly across the bridge; not all the flooring had been installed. At the other side a group of villagers, men and boys of all ages, came to meet us. One offered to carry my camera case. Another carried my leather notebook.

The villagers led us up a narrow, dusty, rock-strewn path. "The road we just left was once a path like this," Essa Khan said. "The new road lets people get their produce to market, but they have had to take it a long way to cross the stream. The new bridge will save them seven kilometers (4.2 miles) of travel."

We walked along a gushing irrigation channel. On our left was the village. It was a collection of one-storey gray stone houses built around an open field, a village common. The path went up a steep hill. Midway to the top, Esa Khan stopped. He pointed proudly to an open shed. Inside, a thick metal pipe ran from the top of the hill to a funnel atop a small orange turbine resting on a table. Black rubber drive belts ran from the turbine to what looked like a large electric motor.

"Come see the generator," Essa Khan said.

We walked to a small shed. A villager was standing inside. He walked to the pipe and turned a valve. Water plunged into the turbine. The generator started turning. The villager pointed to a voltage gauge mounted in a small wooden box atop a wooden post. The needle climbed to 220 volts. A light bulb hanging from a socket attached to a wire hanging from the ceiling lit up in the mid-day sun.

"It works," I said.

"It was just installed," Essa Khan said. "It cost only Rps 20, 000 (then about $1, 000). They brought in an expert to install it. He said it would take seven days, but the villagers were able to do it in three."

"What did you do when you first had electricity?" I asked the villager.

He smiled. "We stayed up until 11 o'clock."

We walked to the village. Six men were spreading a large blanket under a tree. They put thick comforters on the edges for seats. We took off our shoes and sat down. Someone brought trays of sweet white mulberries and succulent red cherries. Essa Khan introduced me to the village leaders. One was Fariq Shah, manager of the village organization which selects and runs the AKRSP projects.

"How did the AKRSP get started here?" I asked.

"At first," Fariq Shah said, "we didn't believe it when someone came from the AKRSP. People had had a bad experience with other agencies that had come here. We thought maybe the AKRSP would cheat us. We thought maybe the Aga Khan wanted our money or that he wanted to convert us from being Shia to being Ismailis."

Hamaran Village was settled in 1940 by people from nearby Bagrote. They had led a hard, confined life, and they were not people who jumped into things. They asked people in other villages about the AKRSP. "We decided that the AKRSP was on the level,"

Fariq Shah said. "A few months later, this was in 1984, we set up a village organization with AKRSP sponsorship. I was elected manager and Hassan Shah, my cousin, was elected president."

"We held meetings with everyone in the village attending, and we decided the first project we wanted to build was another irrigation channel. It would bring water directly from the mountainsides to the fields. We needed to double our agricultural land. We had only about 200 acres. The village had grown to twenty-seven households, almost 200 people.

"The AKRSP agreed to finance the work if we would form a village organization, hold meetings twice a month, and open a savings account. Everyone in the village had to contribute. The books would be open for anyone to inspect. The AKRSP also said it would pay us for our labor."

Paying was a rejection of the widely-held view of other organizations that self-help should mean that people donate their own time and efforts. "That's not much better than forced labor," Shoaib Sultan Khan had told me.

42

On the way back, we stopped at another village, Oshikhandass. The village had been founded by Mir Nazim of Hunza in the early 1930s. Its narrow streets were lined with high stone walls. We stopped at a newly-built gray stone building.

"This is a water treatment plant," Essa Khan told me. "We have built a new water filtration system. Its purity is tested every day by a laboratory in Gilgit. The children of the Aga Khan were here a week ago and they drank it. You should try it."

He filled a glass and handed it to me.

I sipped cautiously. The water tasted fresh and pure, better than the municipal tap water in many cities in the United States. I was thirsty and I drank the rest of the glass eagerly.

We drove into the courtyard of Essa Khan's family house. He led me into a long room with high unpainted wooden beams on the ceiling and tall windows overlooking a veranda that faced a garden. Chairs and couches were lined up against the wall. A bright red Pakistani carpet covered the floor. A woven tapestry of Leonardo da Vinci's painting *The Last Supper* hung on one wall.

A servant brought in lunch: potato, chapatis, rice, and cut up pieces of meat floating in a thick brown curry sauce. I took only a small portion of potatoes, ignoring the meat; I was tired of curry sauces, and I wasn't hungry.

Essa Khan's uncle, Nazim, the village headman and son of the founder, gave me a stern look. "Why no meat? He asked.

I thought for an answer that wouldn't offend him

"I don't eat red meat," I said.

"It's chicken," he said.

I took a small piece. The sauce hid whatever flavor it may have had, and I couldn't eat any more. I felt I had abused their hospitality.

"What do you think of the AKRSP?" I asked.

"It is an honest program," Nazim said. "Here's an example: After we elected a manager of the Village Organization, he used the grant money, Rps 11, 000, to buy himself a watch and liquor and expensive clothing. But the organization's books were open for anyone to see, and the people of the village saw where he had spent the money. They forced him to give it back. He had to sell some of his land to do so. The AKRSP has set up its procedures so that no one can be dishonest."

43

The next day, I went to the AKRSP offices, a short walk from the Chinar Inn. A staff member was waiting to take me to a meeting of a woman's organization.

The women came from villages throughout the area. They ranged in age from their mid-twenties to mid-sixties. They were dressed in their best: embroidered hats, brightly-colored shalwar kameez, veils draped loosely over their heads. Their eyes sparkled.

They were talking about chickens.

One AKRSP program helps village women raise chickens. The AKRSP offers training and one-year loans. The United Nations Development Program supplies the chickens. The women raise the chickens and sell their eggs. The money they earn is their own, perhaps the first money women in their families have ever earned and been able to keep.

I was introduced and I talked briefly about the chickens I had raised as a boy on my parent's farm in Pennsylvania. My father would take the eggs into his office at the *New Yorker Magazine*, where he was executive editor, and sell them for me. It was a nice income for a boy, but I didn't like the chickens. They were dirty and skittish and I had to feed them twice a day, before I went to school and after I came home. On Saturdays, I had to clean out the hen house. It was unpleasant work. I hated it.

I didn't tell the Pakistani women, but a day I still look back on with pleasure was the day when I walked into the hen house after school and found that it was empty and clean.

I ran up the hill to our house.

"Where are the chickens?" I asked my mother.

"They're all in the freezer," she said. "I called Mr. Harrison (the butcher) this morning, and Morris (who helped out around the farm) cleaned out the hen house. You don't need to worry about them any more. From now on, your father and I will give you an allowance."

For the Pakistani women, however, chickens were the first step to self-sufficiency and independence. The joy they felt was reflected in their radiant smiles and exquisite grooming.

44

Pakistanis in the south are fanatical about cricket. In the north, the game is polo. Each village has a polo field. Before we had gone to the polo match in Gilgit, I had told Elfie about the annual polo match at Shandur, one of the world's most unique sporting events. I was sorry that there was no game when we were in Pakistan. The Shandur match is usually held at the end of July.

The first time I went, I almost didn't go.

Riaz had promised to take me, but the managing director of the PTDC had announced he would visit the Northern Areas. Riaz realized he had to stay in Gilgit to meet him. To minimize my disappointment, he had been increasingly negative about the match. He told me no one from Chitral was coming. He told me only a few people from Gilgit would be there. He said the drive was long and uncomfortable. He said the polo played there was not the best. I began not to care about going. I had grown lethargic in the heat of Gilgit and mosquitos had been keeping me awake at night.

Resigned to not going, I went down to breakfast and was surprised when the first person I saw was Saeed, coming out of a room in my path.

"Mr. Shuman," he said. "Do you remember me?"

"Stupid question," I replied, and we embraced.

"Did you come for the polo?" I asked.

"We arrived at five-thirty this morning. We drove all night."

We walked to the lawn. Raja Changez Sultan and Riaz were walking from the parking lot. They had been talking with Shoiab Sultan Khan. We sat in chairs on the lawn. We had talked briefly about the Shandur match over dinner in Rawalpindi. Now he told me more.

"Polo began at Shandur in the 1890's," Saeed said. "Herdsmen would take their sheep and cows and horses to Shandur to graze for the summer. They had little to do, and they began playing polo. The Shandur Polo Tournament actually started in 1937. It was arranged by a British political agent. His name was Evelyn H. Cobb. He was a major in the British army. He was a commanding presence with bristling mustaches, and he was a very, very keen polo player. He even played polo by moonlight. The villagers called him 'Major Mooney.'"

Behind his back. As Margaret Brown, the widow of Major Willie Brown, one of the officers who served under him, later told me, "He wasn't the kind of man you gave nicknames."

"Polo at Shandur died after Partition," Saeed continued. "It was revived in 1986. "It's unique. It's played in the ancient, traditional way."

Our conversation rekindled my interest. I had long liked polo. When my son Jim was three or four years old, my wife and I used to take him to watch polo matches between Army teams at Fort Belvoir, outside Washington, DC.

"Can I ride up to Shandur with you?" I asked Changez and Saeed.

"We have no room," Changez said. "We have to pick up someone in Gupis and the jeep is full of the trophies which will be given to the players."

"Riaz can arrange a jeep and camping equipment," Saeed said.

He did. I left an hour later.

A few miles from Gilgit, the road ran out of pavement. It followed the Gilgit River, turbulent and brown with mud washed from the mountainside by melting glaciers. The river flowed east before it joined the Indus just below Gilgit. Tall, jagged mountains capped by glistening white snow lined both sides.

It was rough country. We crossed swaying suspension bridges. We forded rocky, fast-flowing streams. We passed through villages that were little more than a handful of stone houses and one or two narrow dirt streets, seemingly abandoned except for a storefront or two and, sometimes, one or two people.

Gupis was the largest village. It was once the capitol of one of the Northern Area kingdoms. Now, it was an administrative center. It had two Public Works Department guest houses. I was supposed to spend the night in one of them. My driver stopped the jeep when we reached the center of the village.

"Do you want to continue on to Pfandur?" he asked. It was the next rest house.

"How far is it?"

"Three hours."

I looked at my watch. It was ten after four. "Let's keep going," I said. I knew I could meet up with Saeed and Changez at Pfandur and, if I didn't, I had a tent and my own food.

The Pfandur Public Works Guest House is nine hours by car from Gilgit on the east and three hours from Shandur on the west. I arrived at Pfandur at dusk. The sun had slid behind a dark brown mountain, and children were nudging herds of goats along the narrow road to get home before dark.

The rest house sat atop a high ridge. It was lonely and barren. My driver put up my tent in the forecourt while I wandered through the house. It looked like it hadn't changed since it was built, probably by the British in the 1920's. The furniture was heavy and large and the carpet was threadbare and dirt brown. No one was there, but luggage was scattered about the lounge. I went outside. Behind the house, the ridge dropped sharply to a crystal clear lake, surrounded by other cliffs, like water in a bowl.

Night was coming and I went back to my tent, put on a sweater, turned on my laptop and began typing notes. I was almost finished when Saeed appeared.

"Jim," he said, "we've been fishing. We have fresh trout, if you'd like to join us for dinner."

I did.

I had been longing for fresh fish, but the highlight of the dinner was the water. Changez had brought along a servant who had drawn samples of fresh water from mountain springs. We spent most of the evening sampling and commenting on the different waters like oenophiles at a wine tasting.

The next day, we went fishing. One of the attractions of military service for young British officers in remote Northwest India had been hunting and fishing, and the British had stocked the streams with trout. Changez had simple equipment: a pole made from a long tree branch and a hook baited with a pinch of what appeared to be chappati dough.

As a boy, I had fished with my father. He had a handmade laminated bamboo pole, an expensive English reel, and a hook baited with colorful flies he had carefully tied on long winter weekends. I didn't think Changez would catch many fish with his schoolboy equipment.

Until, that is, he cast his bait into the lake. Within what seemed like seconds, he had a bite. He pulled in a large brown trout. He did it again. And again. And again.

I took an extra pole, wrapped the same bait around the hook and cast for a fish. I waited. And waited. And waited. I never got even a nibble.

Saeed tried. He had no better luck.

Within two hours, Changez had filled two large ice chests with trout.

45

Shandur Pass runs through a green meadow and a lake surrounded by higher mountains. At 12, 500 feet in the Hindu Kush mountains, it is the highest polo field in the world.

To get to Shandur from Pfandur, we passed through tiny mountain villages and finally over a road that was nothing but giant boulders. The road links the eastern – Gilgit – part of Pakistan with the Western part – Chitral.

Our approach to Shandur was dramatically beautiful. The July sun was warm, the countryside was green, streams were flowing clear and fast and the only snow was atop the mountains, a luscious-looking coating that reminded me of the meringue on my grandmother's Christmas pie.

The day before, we had had the road to ourselves. Now, the traffic was unusually heavy: we passed slow-moving jeeps, solitary tractors, tractors pulling farm carts loaded with feed stacks and vegetables and men, who were sitting or standing wherever there was a flat surface. All the work vehicles had been pressed into special service: carrying spectators to Shandur. All the men were singing and laughing.

The road climbed until the altimeter on my Japanese wristwatch read 12, 500 feet. The narrow canyon opened to a broad, hilly, rock-strewn meadow ringed by snow-capped mountains. Two small lakes sparkled like diamonds in the bright sun.

"This is Shandur," my driver said. His face was beaming.

We drove to a camp of tents pitched beside a creek running down the mountain. The people standing by the other tents were not the elegant, moneyed polo crowd of the Western world. Except for a few Westerners like me and a few government officials who arrived in noisy helicopters, most of the people were Pakistani farmers or shopkeepers. They were from Gilgit or Chitral or the isolated small stone villages in between. Yet there was a sense of community. They reminded me of the crowd at an American football game, out for a good game and a good time.

And they loved polo. At dinner beside a campfire, I fell into conversation with a man from Gilgit.

"I'm a radio repairman," he told me, "but I have a polo pony. My wife thinks it is too expensive. My father thinks it is too expensive. But they know how I love it, so they let me keep it."

That evening, there was music and dancing. I went first to see the Chitrali dancers. The Chitralis had sponsored that year's Shandur match and built an enclosure of brightly-colored felt panels on the edge of the polo field. At one end, legs crossed beneath them, sat a six man band. Two musicians played flute-like horns which carried the melody. The four others pounded on drums which provided the rhythm. The music was haunting, plaintive, and hypnotic.

The Chitrali dancers wore white shalwar-kameez and red and green silk vests with the words "Frontier Scouts" embroidered on the back. They performed traditional dances. Their arms and legs swayed to the melody, their feet kept time to the drums. Six men performed a sword dance with polished steel swords and small shields that flashed in the lantern light.

I went looking for Saeed, who had stayed at the camp with Gilgit friends after dinner. The night was dark. There was no moon. Clouds obscured the stars. I had to feel for each footfall as I walked up the mountainside. I heard music and saw the dim flicker of a campfire. I saw people standing in a circle around the fire. I saw Saeed. He joined two other men dancing around the fire. He came back to the circle and we sat together. Other men continued the dancing and one of them pulled me into the circle. I danced, alone, for several minutes, circling the fire, trying to imitate the steps and arm movements I had seen others do. I wondered how out of step I was and whether I was making a fool of myself.

The answer came when a man darted out of the circle and stuck a folded rupee note in my cap. He was followed by three others. I gave the money to the musicians, as is the custom. I didn't look to see how much it was.

The next morning, music woke me. It was unexpected and haunting, a gentle reveille played by flute-like horns accompanied by the quiet rhythm of small drums, and for a moment I wasn't sure where I was. I lay in my sleeping bag listening and letting my eyes adjust to the bright light of the morning sun as it seeped through the thin green walls of the tent. The air was still crisp, and my breath formed small vaporous clouds. Finally, I got up. I dressed quickly and crawled outside.

Four musicians were sitting on the hillside behind the tent. They were dressed in baggy brown and green shalwar kameez. One wore a black sweater with gray elbow patches. Except for their movements, they were almost indistinguishable from the giant moss-covered boulder beside them. The horn players were swaying with the melody. The drummers were raising their arms high above their heads before every beat.

I saw Saeed walking toward me.

"Good morning," he said.

"Salaam alaikum," I replied.

We stood silently and listened to the musicians.

"The music is for the horses and the team," Saeed explained. "It's called Ghalawar music. The musicians have been playing at least two times a day since the horses left Gilgit, a five-day ride. The music gets the horses in the mood for the match."

I looked around, exhilarated by the music and the altitude and the surroundings. The sky was an unblemished blue. Snow-crusted mountains, glistening in the morning sun, surrounded us like the sides of a teacup. A narrow polo field with low stone walls stretched before us. Beyond the field, a dark blue lake sparkled. A rutted dirt road passed the polo field. The road was clogged with dust-covered jeeps and SUVs and tractors pulling wagons packed with standing men. Behind the vehicles, a small band of villagers followed on foot, carrying sacks of clothing and bundles of firewood on their backs. Their faces were beaming in anticipation.

Tents were everywhere. In front of us were the orderly rows of an Army encampment. Scattered everywhere else were a motley collection of big tents and small tents, blue tents and green tents, yellow tents and gray tents. Behind us, beyond the musicians, way up on the steep mountainside, were small dark gray tents and beside them were rumpled men, looking still dazed from sleep, lighting breakfast campfires.

"People camp up there so that they can drink and won't be disturbed," Saeed explained.

I turned around. Behind a rocky hill, an olive-drab military helicopter, carrying VIPs, was noisily landing, stirring up clouds of fine dust.

On my left, horse grooms, dressed in baggy dark brown shalwar kameez and dirt-stained down jackets, were combing the horses. Some of the polo players were already mounted, exercising their horses in the bright morning sunlight.

"Let's get breakfast," Saeed said.

We walked toward a half dozen or so men standing around a waist-high circle of rocks. Inside the circle, under a tattered tan canvas awning, two men were cooking chapatis on hot, flat rocks and spooning porridge onto battered metal plates.

Someone handed me an enamel cup full of hot milk tea. I drank it eagerly, and it took away the morning chill.

We ate our porridge silently.

That morning and afternoon, we watched a B-team match and demonstrations of what once had been war games.

One of the games was tent pegging; horsemen, using long-handled hooks, pulled up tent stakes so that the tents would collapse and smother sleeping soldiers. In another, men on horseback holding long-bladed swords charged at watermelons stuck on wooden poles and cut them in half as though they were the heads of enemies. In still another, men from Gilgit and Chitral engaged in a Herculean tug of war.

That night there was more music and dancing.

The next morning, the sky was overcast. The temperature was in the mid-sixties. Saeed and I walked to the polo field. The field runs perpendicular to the road between two low hills. It is shorter and narrower than the broad playing fields of Western polo and it was covered with scrub grass, with bare spots and an uneven surface. Goal posts wrapped in white and fluorescent pink strips of cotton marked the ends. On each side were two low hills. The larger of the two hills was capped by a red roofed building, built for a visiting Prime Minister. It is controversial.

"Shandur polo is a people's game," I heard one man say. "That building doesn't belong here. Some night we might come up here and blow it up."

The hillside below the pavilion was cut into stone faced terraces, giant steps, on which people sit. The overflow sits on the hillside or on the low stone walls running along each side of the field. If a horse or a ball comes their way, they move out of the way.

We joined Changez and Saleem on the Gilgit side, just below the pavilion. The Gilgit band was sitting on the hillside to our left.

It was playing dance music. A few men were dancing on the field, their arms and bodies moving gracefully. They danced until the players rode onto the field.

Polo at Shandur is fast, competitive, and played in the ancient way: few rules, no time outs, and only a half-time break. In Western polo, each team has four players and a string of horses, one for each quarter. In Northern Pakistan, each team has six players and only one horse per player.

The Chitral players were wearing white polo shirts. The Gilgit players were wearing red. Some of the Chitral players wore polo helmets. The Gilgit players were not protected. None of the horses wore padding.

The music changed. "This is special polo music," Saeed said. "The melodies are associated with the game or with individual players."

The previous year, Gilgit had beaten Chitral 15 to 3, but the B-team match the day before had been close. "Everyone is excited," Saeed told me, 'because this match may be close, too."

The game started with a break from tradition. Usually, a dignitary throws the ball in from the sidelines. This year, someone forgot to designate a dignitary. The referee threw in the ball and the game began.

Two minutes into the game, Gilgit scored the first goal, and the players galloped toward center field to start again. Putting the ball back into play is one of the unique skills required in traditional polo. In Western polo, the referee throws the ball back into play. In Northern Pakistan, the player who scored the goal picks up the ball in his right hand, the same hand that holds the polo stick, and while the band is playing "gallop music," which sounds like a charging horse, he gallops to the center of the field and tosses the ball in the air. Then he hits it with his mallet before it lands on the ground.

"Beautiful," I said.

"This move is called 'Doghar' in Gilgit and 'Tambuk' in Chitral," Saleem explained. Saleem was on the committee to make Shandur an annual event. "Not only is a doghar beautiful to watch, it is central to the game. A well-struck doghar electrifies the game. The most beautiful thing in the game is to see a goal scored by a doghar shot. It is a very proud moment for the player and his team. Players are remembered for the doghars they have hit."

By half-time, the score was 5-0 for Gilgit.

Half-time turned into a party. The band, which seemed to have the endurance of the best polo ponies, kept playing and hundreds of spectators flooded onto the field. Some just stood around, talking. Some danced. Some walked the horses. Some served the players refreshments. "I drink only boiled milk with sugar," one player told me as we stood in the happy crowd. "It is excellent for energy and altitude sickness."

During the second half, I asked Saeed about the origins of polo in Pakistan.

"Polo has deep roots in the Northern Areas," he told me. "The game originated in Central Asia more than 2, 500 years ago. It spread through China to Tibet and the northeast of India and to Gilgit and Chitral through Baltistan, which was once the most western part of the Tibetan Empire. In those days, everyone had horses and everyone began playing polo. The rulers – the Mirs and the Methars and the Rajas – liked the game so much that they spent half the state's income supporting it. The word "polo" is Tibetan. It came from Baltistan, and it means ball. The British first saw the game in the Eastern part of India in the mid-1800's and brought it back to England. From there it spread to the United States and to the rest of the world.

"Two of the matches here at Shandur have been attended by Prime Ministers," Saeed added. "Gen. Zia-ul-Haq came in 1986, and Benazir Bhutto came in 1989."

After a half hour, the referee blew a whistle. Gilgit had won 9-0. The Gilgit band began playing victory music. Spectators rushed onto the field. Some picked up Gilgit players and carried them on their shoulders. Others danced beneath them. The sky was punctuated with unopened umbrellas, brandished like swords of victory.

Awards were presented and people began to leave. At polo festivals in villages, people party far into the night. Not one lives near Shandur and everyone wanted to start for the long journey home. The narrow road through the pass filled quickly.

Changez had invited me to ride back with him. We missed connections, but I was able to hitch a ride in a jeep with two young women from New Zealand and a backpacker from Northern England. In every village, women and children lined the streets or sat on rooftops to watch the parade that was passing by. The women were wearing their best jewelry, silver and turquoise necklaces and bracelets that could have come from expensive shops selling American Indian jewelry in Arizona or New Mexico.

As we passed by, the women cheered and shouted "Pakistan Zindabad." Shandur Polo was part of their lives too, even if they hadn't been to the match.

Remembering the game years later, I was sorry that Elfie had not been there. She had missed a unique event.

46

Back in Gilgit, after the Shandur polo match, I continued to talk with Mr. Riaz about the history and customs of Hunza. One morning, he came up to me at breakfast.

"I am going to Aliabad," he said. "It is my home village. Would you like to come? It's for festivities marking the coronation date of the Aga Khan."

Aliabad is one of the towns of Hunza, down the hillside from Altit and Baltit. We left at five o'clock. I ate dinner alone, read for a while, and went to bed early.

The next morning, Riaz met me at my room and took me across the KKH to the center of Aliabad. We stopped at the Domini Inn. Riaz and his family own the inn. His brother manages the inn and a small store which sells gems and Hunza handicrafts. Riaz and his brother chatted for a few minutes.

Riaz pointed to a man in a Hunza cap and sunglasses sitting in the sun on a balcony. "That is my father," he said. "He lives with my brother." Riaz waved to the man, who smiled and waved back.

We walked down a narrow street that ended in a garden full of Army tents. "This is our campground," Riaz explained. "It is part of the hotel. The tents have beds and there is a toilet building for men and another for women."

Earlier, I had told him I wanted to see an ancient religious ceremony in which a Shaman, called the Bityan, dances and communes with the fairies (gods), and foretells the future of the village. I had agreed to pay the Bityan's fee and to pay for the musicians and the goat which would have to be slaughtered at the beginning of the ceremony. It would cost me $60.

"If we have the Bityan ceremony," Riaz said, "it will be here." He touched the leaves of a walnut tree, heavy with round, green walnuts. "The fairies like the walnuts," Riaz said. "They come down from the mountains through the trees."

The grounds where the village festival was to be held were about half a mile away. As we walked through the narrow streets of the village, people greeted Riaz like a returning hero. Several, men and women, kissed his hand.

We walked past a building so small it could have been a child's playhouse. Elaborate wood carving decorated the posts and doorways. "This is the old mosque," Riaz explaine. Two small boys were using the platform in front to sell cold sodas and packaged biscuits.

We entered the grounds of the large and imposing new mosque, and passed onto the festival grounds set on a terraced hillside overlooking Rakaposhi. We sat on a carpet under the shade of an awning strung from the trees. The hillside behind us was filling with women and young children. The women were dressed in bright colors, reds and oranges and yellows. The children looked freshly scrubbed. They were wearing freshly-laundered clothes, shorts or shalwar kameez for the boys and dresses for the girls. Most of the small children had makeup around their eyes. One small girl, with red hair and rouge on her fair skin, looked as luscious as a peach.

Older boys rushed around in groups of three or four, looking for friends or a better place to sit or for whatever prompts small boys to run around at village festivals anywhere in the world.

Wardens wearing bronze badges tried to keep order by waving heavy lathi sticks and shouting. The man in charge of the public address system tried to get it working, and kept saying "hello, hello" into the microphone.

We heard a band playing. Two men beating large bass drums came through the gate at the top of the garden. They were followed by a man blowing a horn. The band walked to a space under a tree to our right. A procession of villagers followed. At the head of the procession were the village elders. They sat on the mats beside us.

"They are all remarkable men," Riaz told me softly. One of them was his father, whom we had seen sitting on a balcony a few hours before. He was tall and gentle. His grandfather had been Mir of Hunza in the 19th Century, and he, himself, had been headman of the village.

The wardens tried to sort out the crowd. Small boys had taken over the best seats and the wardens told them to move. Riaz suggested that we, too, move to the other side. "There is shade there," he said.

We moved and the band began playing, again. One of the village elders began dancing. He was given a Hunza cloak with sleeves half again as long as his arms and a red flower embroidered on the back. The man danced well, and several men in the audience rose to stick rupee notes in the band of his hat. Soon other old men and some of the distinguished men of the village – Riaz among them – joined in the dancing. And then others, young and old, began dancing.

The music stopped. A man came up to me. He said something in Burushaki, the language of Hunza which has no roots or words in common with any other language.

"He wants you to dance," Riaz translated. "You are a distinguished guest. I told the people in the village that you were a high official of the Aga Khan Foundation. Will you dance?"

I borrowed a hat, for I had been told that "people who dance without hats are like orphans" and I went out to the cleared space. The band began playing. I didn't try to do a dance, as I had done at Shandur. I began dancing to the beat and the melody. I lost myself in the music and I was aware only of the music and the green of the trees. People began applauding. I danced until I was tired, and then I gave the band Rps 100 and went back to my seat.

"That was good, very good," Riaz said, obviously pleased.

More dancing followed. The villagers fell away when sword dancers, waving small metal shields painted with a thin white-wash, entered the circle. As they danced, their swords caught the rays of the sun seeping through the trees, sending bright splashes of light into the crowd. They were followed by a game of musical chairs. Rocks substituted for chairs. One player thought he had figured out a way to beat the system. He began kicking the rock, like a soccer ball, so that it would always be close when the music stopped. The other players soon saw this and objected. A referee stopped him. He lost a few rounds later.

Next was weight lifting. The weight was a large gasoline can full of water. Four men held onto an iron rod stuck through the can's handles and tried to lift it. They couldn't get it off the ground.

There were several games of tug of war, using a thick brown rope with a pink ribbon tied in the center. The men on each side wore heavy cloaks to protect their backs if they fell. Their feet dug into the black dirt and for several minutes the rope didn't move in either direction. Only when the side to my left grew tired did the other side win.

The festival ended. As Riaz and I walked away, he asked me, "Would you mind if we held the Bityan ceremony this afternoon? It will be impossible to do it on July 25th. "There should be no music during Moharram [The Muslim New Year's Day]."

"Then let's do it this afternoon," I answered.

We had lunch sitting at a table outside. It was served by Riaz' mother, a thin, jolly looking woman.

Then, Riaz and I walked to the camp ground. He introduced me again to the village elders, More than a dozen had come. One was Riaz' father. Their eyes sparkled in anticipation.

The men made room for me at the front. "You are the guest of honor," Riaz said. "You should have the best seat."

The band began playing.

"The music will attract the people," Riaz explained. The small crowd drawn there by the announcement at the end of the morning festival began to grow.

A warden with a stick in his hand and a feather in his cap appeared and began moving a group of women back from the open circle. A few men began to dance. Within a few minutes, the crowd had grown to more than a hundred people. We waited.

"The Bityan will be here soon," Riaz assured me. "I sent a jeep for him."

The warden began encouraging the people sitting in the circle to cheer, like the warm-up act for a TV show.

A man led a small brown goat to me. The goat looked at me without curiosity. It put its head down and began eating grass. I stroked its back. Its hair was smooth as silk. A small boy next to me reached out and touched the goat's horns. The goat kept eating the grass.

"The Bityan has arrived," Riaz announced. His face was full of delight. A man came through the crowd and picked up the goat. I was relieved. I had been afraid that I would have to cut the goat's throat.

A slightly-built man with high cheek bones came up to me. In his right hand, he held a leather carry-all bag. He was wearing white shoes and an aquamarine shalwar-kameez. He wore his hair long in the back.

"This is Ibrahim, the Bityan," Riaz said. "He is the best Bityan in Hunza. He is from Altit village."

"Salaam aleikum," I said.

He shook my hand and smiled. His teeth were a brilliant white.

People in the crowd saw him and began cheering. He walked through the center of the circle and disappeared into the crowd. The band kept playing, but the men who were dancing faded back into the crowd.

Ibrahim came back into the circle from the side opposite me. He was now wearing a long homespun white robe with red lining on its outer edges. The sleeves hung down to his knees. He danced to the band and stuck his head into smoke from incense burning on a tin dinner plate. It was juniper. Some of the smoke drifted to me, and I could smell its clear vapors.

Ibrahim continued to dance. His eyes became glazed. A man standing beside the band handed him the goat's severed head. Ibrahim put the neck to his mouth and sucked the blood as he danced around the circle. He held the head away from his face as though making an offering to the fairies. His lips and chin were red with fresh blood. His eyes were glazed in ecstasy.

"The fairies like blood," Riaz explained. "It is like mother's milk to them."

Ibrahim tossed the goat's head over the heads of the crowd and into the field behind them. He danced up to one of the drums and put his head down beside it.

"He is listening for the fairies in the drum," Riaz said.

The crowd was cheering, but I could hear Ibrahim singing.

"He is singing what the fairies told him," Riaz said.

Ibrahim danced away from the drum. His eyes were blank and his face looked happy. He returned to the drum, bent his body down, listened to the rhythm, and began singing. He danced away from the drum.

Suddenly, a young man broke into the open circle. He was wearing a dirty white shalwar kameez and black sandals, and he began dancing. His movements were younger, more energetic, but his eyes were glazed. He danced around the circle, his face transposed.

Ibrahim seemed unaware of him.

"He is the new Bityan," Riaz said. "His name is Karim."

Karim danced toward the drum and put his head down, as Ibrahim had done. Ibrahim was dancing on the opposite side of the circle. Suddenly, he fell to the ground. I thought he had died. Three men grabbed him as he fell and carried him away.

Karim danced around the circle for three or four minutes. His eyes were lifted to the skies and his hands were outstretched. He stopped only when four men on the edge of the crowd grabbed him and pulled him away. He was still in a state of ecstacy.

"Karim is the new Bityan," Riaz said, "but his family does not like that. They think it is all silly superstition. He goes into a trance whenever he hears the music."

Riaz summoned one of the drummers, a man in his late forties with a sun wrinkled face.

"What did the Bityan sing?" I asked.

"He said the fairies prophesy that this will be a blessed year for the village and a prosperous year." He paused. "And for the foreigners, he says the fairies say the same thing. The foreigners' minds are in transit, but they will have a blessed and prosperous year."

It was not a startling prophecy, but the crowd was in high spirits as they dispersed.

47

The next day, I went to talk with Ibrahim. He lived in a stone house perched on a terraced hillside on the road to Altit. When I arrived, he was sitting on the terrace wall in the shade of a tree.

A translator, Saki Ahmed Jan, had arranged the interview, and we followed Ibrahim into a small room. It was furnished with four chairs, a table, and a bed on which eight mattresses were rolled up. Ibrahim's Bityan coat hung on a nail just below the ceiling beams.

We moved the chairs so that Ibrahim and I sat next to each other. Saki Ahmed Jan sat across from us. Ibrahim spoke in Burushaski. Saki Jan's English was a bit sketchy, but here is the interview as I transcribed it:

"I have been a Bityan since 1944, when I was fifteen. It happened to me on the 25th of June, which was a holiday, a family day. I was a shepherd, herding sheep and goats in a mountain pasture above Altit, and I left my herd to collect flowers, which is what people did on that day. I picked flowers and put them into my cap, a Hunza cap with sides that roll down. I sat on a rock and I felt my senses spinning. I didn't know it was the rock where the fairies live. I fell on the stone and, later, when I opened my eyes I saw a lot of fairies looking

at me. They looked like European women with long hair and light skin and straight nose. But their feet were on backward. They were dressed in bright colors, red, green, white, yellow. One was named Subyan. She was Queen of the Fairies, and she was wearing green, the color of tree leaves, and an embroidered shirt.

"I went back to sleep, and when I woke up the fairies were gone. I felt happy. I saw my sheep and goats very far way. It was getting dark, so I whistled for them and they came running. I knew the fairies were helping me.

"The other shepherds and I went into the shepherds' house and found cheese and yogurt and bread and butter. It was all ready to eat, and we ate and went to sleep.

"We returned to Altit early the next morning and we brought the flowers and the food the fairies had brought. In the village, we saw the musicians playing on the polo ground and people were dancing. A man named Moghul, who was area secretary for the King, asked who we shepherds were. The people said we were good people, and he told the band to play music for us.

"The band began playing Shirzawan music, the music of the fairies, and I started to dance to that music. People started cheering and I felt three rays of light sit on my shoulder. I knew they were fairies and they told me to dance.

"The people who were watching me said, 'Ibrahim looks crazy. He has been drinking Hunza water [wine]. He's crazy.'

"Moghul looked into my face and said, 'It looks like he has fairies.'

"Moghul had people carry me to the musicians, and he told the musicians to play fairy music. I started dancing and the people knew I was was with good fairies, that I was a good Bityan.

"Moghul went to tell the king. 'Good dancing and good fairies, Mr. Ibrahim.'"

"The king sent people to Altit and told them to make a program for the Bityan and give him goat blood. And the King watched and said I was good.

"The King asked for another dance. This one was to be in Karimabad, in Baltit Fort, his palace. He had a dancing dress made for me, white shoes, white trousers, and a green shirt. Someone brought a goat and cut its throat and gave me the head. I drank the blood. The blood is like mother's milk to the fairies.

"I performed three ceremonies. If I had not done it three times there would have been big trouble for my health and body.

"Then the fairies carried me to the mountain where I had first seen them. I lived there for seven days and they gave me for breakfast, lunch, and dinner only one cup of milk from a Marco Polo sheep.

"The people in the village noticed I was missing, and they went to tell the King. The King said, 'Bring all the musicians to one place and have them play loudly and build a big fire for good smell. With sweet music and good smell, the fairies will bring Ibrahim down.'

"When I heard the music I came to my senses.

"The fairies told me, 'The people are calling; they make music.'

"I got up. The fairies helped me over the big rocks and bad places. When I got to the village, I jumped out from behind the musicians and started dancing. To make me stop, the people put water to my face, and I was all right. That is the end of my story."

Ibrahim said that the good fairies look like Europeans. They make people healthy and make crops and animals flourish. Bad fairies, who have "very dark faces" make people sick and kill people. The fairies speak in Shina, the language of Gilgit. Ibrahim speaks only Burusheski, the Hunza language, "but when I am dancing," Ibraham told me, "Shina seems like my own language."

He dances whenever invited. Recently, this had been about six times a year. Normally, he is a farmer.

There have been seven Bityans in the Hunza tradition. The tradition may end with Ibrahim. Karim's parents strongly oppose his becoming a Bityan and he has performed only one full ceremony of his own, drinking goat's blood. But he may have the fairy possession. Ibrahim said he cannot dance when Karim is dancing, and I wondered if the prophetic tradition, the ancient form of religion, continues if the man chosen to continue it cannot. Or will another man, or woman – for there have been female Bityans — be chosen?

48

The next morning, on the way back to Gilgit, I asked Berham, "Is there still a Bityan ceremony?"

"No," he said dismissively, "we don't have that anymore."

I was disappointed. An ancient Hunza tradition had died.

49

Elfie and I looked forward to a day of rest at the Serena Lodge.

At dinner, we sat at a table across from a group of young Italians, casually but elegantly dressed. The men were wearing indigo jeans and sport shirts, the one woman was wearing a colorful shalwar kameez. She was the wife of one of the men.

"We live in Kathmandu," her husband told me. "We are working on a United Nations project recording local history, planning parks, preserving wildlife. These areas are changing so quickly that much of what made them unique will soon be lost."

They were delighted to learn that Elfie was originally from Switzerland.

"We're from Rome," the woman said. "My mother lives near the Swiss-Italian border on Lake Lugano."

"It is a beautiful area," I said. "It's Elfie's favorite Canton. Elfie has been to San Nazzaro often. I've been there only once but I loved it."

When we returned to our room, I asked Elfie "Do you still want to fly back to Islamabad?" We had made plane reservations a few days before.

"Driving the KKH is the experience of a lifetime," Elfie replied. "But once is enough. Besides, we've been invited to Hannah Rehman's wedding."

50

We flew back to Islamabad on the morning plane. Before we could board, we had to wait in segregated waiting rooms. Elfie got into conversation with a school teacher. Her husband and son were with the men. I sat alone and watched the men in the waiting room. Interesting faces, I thought.

Suddenly, I was asked to follow an airline official who led me to the plane before the others. Elfie walked behind the women, all colorfully-dressed. She took last minute photographs of the trailing shawls, the majestic mountains, the airfield, the small plane, and Shabir waving to us from outside the fence.

Berham had arranged for first class seats. That meant the first two seats behind the pilots' cabin, facing all the passengers. When the plane climbed steeply, Elfie was afraid she would fall on the man across from her even though she was wearing a seat belt. She laughed so hard she had to hide her face in her shawl.

The plane followed the mountain canyons, sometimes at eye level with the mountain ridges, sometimes a few hundred feet below. The view of the rumpled and parched mountains was spectacular, and it was a lot more comfortable than sitting in the backseat of the SUV for two days.

Adam met us at the airport.

"I've seen only one policeman," I said as we walked to the parking lot. "The city seems quiet. I thought there would be more tension under the 'State of Emergency.'"

"We are a peaceful people," Adam said.

We returned to the Hunza Embassy Lodge. Dark blue police buses and swarms of uniformed police lined the street. Harried men carrying cameras and notebooks rushed past us.

"What's going on?" I asked Adam.

"Benazir has a house near here," he said.

Benazir Bhutto had returned to Pakistan from her home in Dubai a few weeks before. Terrorists had attacked her motorcade as it was driving to a rally in Karachi. At least 139 people were killed and 450 injured. A few days later she had come to Islamabad and was planning to make a speech at Liaquat Park in Rawalpindi. For safety reasons, the speech was canceled and she was put under house arrest.

As soon as the car stopped, we heard a strong, beautiful woman's voice speaking in Urdu over a loudspeaker. People were cheering and shouting, "Pakistan Zindabad, Benazir Zindabad. Pakistan Zinabad. Benazir Zindabad."

I turned to Adam. "Who's speaking," I asked.

"It's Benazir," he replied. "The garden of her house backs up to the garden of the Hunza Lodge. She's speaking to the people in the street."

We rushed to our room and turned on the television, hoping to see her. The TV showed only a man and a woman, commentators, sitting behind a desk.

Disappointed, we turned off the TV. We listened through open windows, joining in spirit the crowd we could not join physically.

"So much for promising our friends not to go anywhere near Benazir or demonstrations," Elfie said.

51

Saleem and Shauki invited us to dinner. While we were talking with the other guests, Shauki drew Elfie aside.

"Would you come with me for a moment?" she asked softly.

They entered a bedroom in which two men were waiting. They were Shauki's tailor and an assistant. They had come to take Elfie's measurements to make her some Pakistani clothes, and they had brought some beautiful fabrics to chose from.

Elfie was stunned.

"Thank you," she said, turning to Shauki. "This is incredibly kind of you. I don't know how to thank you enough."

Shauki smiled and they went back to the main part of the house.

Two days later, two beautiful shalwar kameez were delivered to our room at the Hunza Embassy Lodge.

52

The next evening we went to Major and Mrs. Rehman's house on Rawal Lake for the wedding of their daughter Hannah.

Adam drove us.

Saleem, his wife, Shauki, and their son, Taimur, were waiting for us in their SUV by the side of the road. We followed them. Although we were in the city of Islamabad, the area was sparsely settled, dry, and desolate. We passed only a few houses, all of them large, and here and there a store. We passed A.Q. Khan Road, named for the father of Pakistan's atomic bomb, who was under house arrest for selling nuclear secrets to North Korea and other countries.

Adam turned down a rutted dirt road and let us out at the driveway of the Rehmans' house. Major and Mrs. Rehman were standing by the gate welcoming guests. Saleem parked his car and joined us in the driveway. He led us to the large side garden, covered by a huge tent. Adam followed.

Red Oriental carpets covered the grass. Several hundred chairs faced a brightly decorated platform on which the bride and groom would sit. Directly in front of the platform was a dance floor. Serving tables topped with steel warming pans lined the rear of the tent. Small lights hung from the tent poles. Flowers were everywhere. A band was playing.

Elfie looked around the tent, decorated in yellow and gold. Everywhere were beautiful women in exquisite shalwar kameez or saris and wearing elegant jewelry.

"It's a thousand and one nights atmosphere," Elfie whispered to me. "I wonder if photographs will do it justice. It's exotic, almost unreal."

Saleem's wife, Shauki, led Elfie to the women's section and introduced her. Saleem and I sat on folding chairs in the men's section.

The night was cold. Saleem and I went inside to the library. In honor of the wedding, a bar was set up at the back of the room. Someone brought us each a half-filled glass of Scotch.

"Would Elfie like some wine?" Saleem asked.

"I'm sure she would," I answered.

He broke away from our group.

Elfie, later on, told me that she was surprised to suddenly be confronted by a man bringing her "a gift," as he called it. A bit confused, she looked into the women's faces, wondering if she should accept a glass of wine.

The women smiled and encouraged her. Most of them had visited or studied abroad. Elfie said she hesitated but felt so cold in her silk shalwar kameez that she was grateful for the warmth of the red wine.

Standing with the men, I began talking with Saleem's brother, Saeed Malik.

"What can be done to save Pakistan?" I asked.

"All this terrorism could be stopped if someone set up a Sufi university," he said. "Sufism is a peaceful sect."

After some time, the groom arrived, escorted by his friends. We went outside. Candles flickered on the tables. The guests were talking quietly, waiting with anticipation for the bride. She entered, walking under a canopy, surrounded by beautiful young women. Her face was hidden by a veil. Her friends showered her with flower blossoms. She climbed to the stage and sat in a chair beside the groom. Their parents, brothers, and sisters stood beside them.

The henna celebration, in which her hands were painted with elegant designs, had already taken place, and the marriage contract had been signed the day before. Tonight, on the first evening of the celebrations, an ancient tradition, dating from the time of arranged marriages, was reenacted. She held up her hand and looked at her future husband through a tiny mirror in the ring on her finger. In arranged marriages, it would be the first time the bride would see her husband. It didn't apply here.

"Of course, they knew each other," Mrs. Rehman told Elfie. "Parents now try to be more understanding and let the youngsters have a word in the matter."

The band resumed playing. The dance floor filled with people, mostly women and children. They danced enthusiastically. Elfie joined them.

Dinner was announced. I joined Elfie in the buffet line. Waiters in white jackets served the food. The fragrance of the food, with its varied spices, made my mouth water.

When our plates were full, Elfie smiled at me and went back to a festively decorated table with the women she had been sitting with before. I sat with Saleem and some of the other men in another section.

Occasionally, I would meet Elfie's eyes across the room, and we would smile.

Later, we all got a glimpse of the bride's face, still mostly hidden. This night she would remain at her parent's home, without the groom. They would leave together the following night.

The party went late into the night. We arrived back at the Hunza Embassy Lodge at 2:00 in the morning.

53

Early the next afternoon, Elfie and I went to buy some books at the Saeed Book Bank in the Jinnah Supermarket. A small blue van was parked on the street. A sign painted on its side read: "This nation is time delayed."

54

The second night of the three-night wedding ceremony was even more elegant than the first night. It was more formal. The tent beside the Rehman's house had been redecorated with new colors and fresh flowers. Elfie and I entered and talked with other guests until the young couple entered. Friends escorted them to a golden platform, where they sat together as newly-weds and graciously accepted everyone's good wishes.

Hannah was dressed in an elaborate, subtly-colored long gown. Jewelry sparkled on her bare arms. She was smiling beatifically. Her husband was wearing a black suit, with a white shirt and a tan necktie. They were surrounded by family and friends as their guests mounted the platform and sat beside them for wedding pictures. We took our turn. Elfie looked especially elegant.

There was music and dancing.

Then came the climatic moment. The groom took his bride's hand to leave her parent's house and follow him to his family. Wedding guests walked with the couple to their lavishly decorated car. I saw tears in Mrs. Rehman eyes as she walked with her daughter. The ceremony represented the passage of a young woman leaving her parent's house to become a wife and part of her husband's family. It was emotional and touching, acknowledging the symbolic value of this important step from maidenhood to womanhood.

The next day, Sunday, a party was given at the groom's house to welcome the bride. We had a previous engagement and could not attend. We were disappointed. On Monday, the bride and groom would leave for their honeymoon in Turkey, "abroad" as they called it.

A few days later, Elfie was delighted when Mrs. Rehman told her that she had heard from the young couple. "Will Hannah live with her in-laws?" Elfie asked.

"No," Mrs. Rehman said, "they have their own place."

55

The next day, Raja Changez Sultan invited us for lunch. I had last seen him more than a decade before when I stayed in his house after I had arrived in Islamabad late at night after a long trek on horseback through Kyrgyzstan.

Changez is one of Pakistan's most noted artists, an internationally known painter and poet. He is former head of the National Council on the Arts, which was set up in 1973 to promote the visual and performing arts in Pakistan.

He was sitting on a swinging bench on the lawn.

A servant brought a pitcher containing a fruit drink. We chatted about our lives since we had last met.

"I've never forgotten your prowess as a fisherman," I told him. "Before Elfie and I left for Pakistan I looked in novelty stores to bring you a joke gift: a rubber fish. I hadn't been able to find one."

Lunch was announced, and we went into the house. The walls were bare.

"The house is being painted," Changez explained.

Changez's wife, Azra, came downstairs.

He pulled back some canvases lined against a desk in his office. Some were part of his widely-praised series, *Himalayan Odyssey,* mystical paintings of mountains. "There is also poetry with it," he said. He opened a gray laptop computer and inserted a disk.

Music started. A painting of snow-dotted brown mountains appeared on the screen.

"The Himalayan Odyssey," the voice over began. It was Changez' voice. "The mind is on a trek through rugged mountains in despair/ such desolation/ such unglamorous terrain..."

The pictures changed, showing the play of light on mountains. "The high peaks of the Karakoram rise...the mighty Indus bursts its barrier..."

Changez turned off the laptop. "I'll make you a copy," he said.

"I didn't know you were a poet, too," I said.

"The Chinese believed an artist should be a writer as well as a painter," he said.

We sat down to lunch, and talked about the flourishing arts in Pakistan. Changez recited more poetry, and when we left, he invited Elfie to exhibit her paintings in his gallery in Karachi.

56

That afternoon, we went to the home of Rear Admiral (Retd.) Mian Zahir Shah, his wife, Nasira, and their two daughters. We wanted to meet with a group of what Saleem and Saeed had described as "powerful women." The women sat in the living room in a circle, on chairs, couches, even the piano bench.

Many women in Pakistan hold powerful jobs. Benezir Bhutto, after all, had been Prime Minister. We wondered what life was like for such women in a heavily male-oriented society.

"How difficult is it for a woman to have a career in Pakistan?" I asked.

The first to speak was Shabnam Riaz, who was sitting opposite me on the piano bench. She had grown up in London and was now a television news presenter for Pakistan's national television network, PTV World. She is also a poet. General Musharraf wrote the foreword to her first book of poems, *The Whispering Wind*.

"It is definitely a balancing act," she said. "It's very difficult being a professional woman in Pakistan."

Next to speak was Zupash Imran, a London-trained lawyer in her thirties. She was wearing a female version of the uniform of Pakistani lawyers: a black jacket and dress, a white shirt and a black and white stripped tie.

"We are the privileged class, women with strong links to the middle class and the establishment," she said. "Less is expected of women here. Men have an innate, inherent respect for women. The only problem I had was that men attempted to denigrate our gender. But that is easing now. It makes it easier for younger women. Now there are a lot of female lawyers. But we have a responsibility. We need to empower more middle class women."

Jasmeela Aslam, also a lawyer, added "Nobody does anything to empower the middle class." She said she had been teaching birth control. "We need to get the government to support us," she said. "Women are very receptive. Men are not. They say children are God's gift."

Sadia Syed, who does development work in remote villages, talked of other problems. "There is still violence against women" she said. "There are 'kitchen fires' where women are burned to death by in-laws. It is such a problem that twice a year a group of doctors from France come to Pakistan to help the badly-burned victims. But I'm teaching the 'modern world.' My mother had five daughters. We were tomboys. We'd wrestle with boys, walk on marbles. I was not raised to be anybody special, so I consider myself to be ordinary. I want kids with money to see the other side. I have adopted children for education. In small villages, I installed tube wells. The wells became a community center for gossip. They were like clubs for women. They also created a common awareness, pride in their homes, cleanliness. They were so successful that my maid give me one hundred rupees to put in a tube well."

Elfie asked if women could get divorced. In Islam, a man can divorce his wife simply by saying three times, "I divorce you."

One of the lawyers answered. "Interestingly enough, the women in the tribal areas are much more aware of their property rights and know exactly what they have brought into a marriage. I have seen many lists: One bed, three blankets, four plates, two pots, et cetera. And, they are keenly aware of their rights should a marriage fail. Their life is often a struggle, lived under hardship and in the most difficult circumstances."

Shaheen Shehzada is an artist who has lived much of her life outside Pakistan. "I had a Bohemian background," she said. "I spent 27 years in America and the West. Can I do what I want? Of course I can, and who would stop me." But, she added, "education is the crux of the matter in this country."

Dr. Rubina Akhter is a noted plant biologist. She holds a PhD from Vienna University. She has spent the past twenty years working on conservation-oriented projects in all areas of Pakistan, from the deserts of Sindh to the Karakoram mountains.

"I've been to villages where people have never seen any cars," she said. "I've been in places where women carry all the load on their back; the men carry only a gun. But men are becoming interested in the role of women. Some want their daughters to be doctors. We are not the third world."

Naureen Butt worked for a Non-Governmental Organization, which looks after street children, children with HIV, and children forced into prostitution. "Why does the media not give us the true picture?" she asked. "It was not planned, this rivalry that is going on in the world. The media, satellite dishes and television, show there is a world beyond the village. It's really a global village. People are bringing change themselves. You've got to make them feel you are a part of them."

She had a suggestion. "You should visit a school for street kids," she said. She suggested one in Rawalpindi.

57

The school is called Rah-e-Amal.

We arrived the next afternoon. On the way, we passed an encampment of people living in faded green army tents. For many, Rawalpindi is a city of bare survival. We saw small girls taking care of naked infants, sitting on dirty mattresses beside tattered army tents with dented plastic jerry cans of water resting on the dirt beside them. One young woman was sitting on a folding cot tending a cooking fire.

The students we were about to meet were the lucky ones.

Shabir parked the car beside a sprawling white house, and we walked to a large yard in the rear. The students were in their classes, sitting on mats on a parched field. Blackboards rested on portable easels. The school was co-educational; girls sat next to boys in each class.

"That's unusual," I said. "Co-education in Pakistan."

"We thought that boys and girls should learn to get along and respect each other," Zehra, who had started the school, said. "It will help them later in life, as adults."

"How did you start this school," I asked.

"It's a long story but a successful one," she replied. "One day, an old man knocked at my door and asked me if I could keep two of his grandchildren. He said his daughter was about to sell them. They were four and five years old. I did not know how to react at first. I remember looking out my window and thinking with sadness what a waste that these children would have no chance in life. I got some friends together and we decided to start a school for severely-deprived children. My hope was that we could raise enough money so that the children or their parents would have to pay nothing. Tuition, books, stationary, meals, uniforms, and medical care would be provided free. We would give them a nourishing meal at mid-day. We knew that giving them money for food would not work because, in most cases, the families would demand it and let the children go hungry. I wanted to emphasize character building, developing humanitarian values, and to create a culture of peace and tolerance. I wanted to channel the students' energy towards positive thinking so that we could build a better civil society, one devoid of violence and other ills."

Inside the house, over tea, she showed us photographs of the first students as they grew older. Many who once had no hope for any kind of career, are now applying to colleges. One example stuck in my mind.

Before he began attending the Rah-e-Amal school, one boy thought he would be a "sweeper" like his father. He had only one ambition. He hoped to be a "sweeper" for a large corporation. The working conditions would be better than his father's. And the job might be steady. As he began to get an education, he changed. One day, he saw President Musharraf on television. It triggered a realization of his own potential. "The president has two legs. I have two legs," he told one of his teachers. "The president has two arms. I have two arms. Why couldn't I be president?"

Now, he plans to attend law school.

58

As we left, I asked if the State of Emergency had affected the school. "It has one effect," one of the teachers said. "We realized that the government has failed to do anything for Pakistan. One thing about the State of Emergency is that we are learning that we can't trust in government. We'll have to do it ourselves."

59

That night, Elfie and I invited people who had helped us to dinner. We met in an upstairs room at Pappasallis Italian Restaurant in Islamabad.

"We'd like to thank you all for your incredible hospitality and your generosity in letting us be part of your life. You have made this visit an unforgettable and joyous experience," Elfie said. "I hope to return some day."

"Elfie, we hope you'll come back," Saleem said. He looked at me with a smile. He had told me earlier in the trip that he and Saeed had often wondered if I would come back to Pakistan.

Now, he told Elfie, "You can even bring Jim."

60

Back in Lahore, we spent a day in one of Lahore's oldest markets, buying shawls and handicrafts to be sold at fund raisers for the Afghan Refugee Girls School.

Elfie was selective. She enjoyed the task. She bargained while sipping tea, not hurried, graciously accepting the social exchange of pleasantries. Her gift with people eased the bargaining with the merchants and we left with a full duffel case.

That evening, Shabir and Arshad drove us to the airport. Elfie embraced Shabir.

"Goodbye, my dear Hunzakut," she said, using the endearing name for the people of Hunza which Elizabeth Lorimer had used in her book.

"I'm now looking for a European wife," Shabir said.

Elfie laughed. She remembered Peshawar, when she had asked if she was too Western, and they both Arshad and Shabir had remained silent.

Now, as we gathered our luggage together under the airport lights, we were sad, For us, it was a sorrowful departure. We could feel that Arshad and Shabir felt as sad as we did.

We walked into the airport terminal, looking back and waving.

The airport was a surprise. Unlike the terminal I remembered which looked like something built hastily during World War II, it was new, modern, and spacious, and it was named after Muhammad Iqbal.

After we had checked in, Elfie turned to me. "It's been a long day," she said. "The first thing I will do when we get to New Delhi is to take a relaxing hot shower and then hit the bar."

"I can't wait for my first sip of Laphroaig," I said. "I've missed the smoky taste of an Islay single malt."

"On second thought," she said, "maybe, my shower can wait until I go to bed. Let's have that drink first."

Shortly after our plane was airborne, the pilot announced that we were the last flight allowed to leave Lahore because of restrictions unexpectedly imposed under the state of emergency. Pakistan was still unsettled.

Postscript

A few weeks after we left, Benezir Bhutto was assassinated after delivering a speech in Rawalpindi. Less than a year later, Gen. Musharraf, facing threat of impeachment, resigned and Benazir's husband, Asif Ali Zardari, became President.

Pakistan remained contentious and unstable. The United States intensified the fight against the Taliban and Al Queda, attacking tribal areas in the west using drone bombers controlled from as far away as Nevada. The attacks fueled anti-American riots in Peshawar, Lahore, Karachi, and Rawalpindi. So, too, did the killing of Osama bin Laden, the terrorist leader long sought by the United States. He was killed by a team of U.S. Navy Seals in a house in Abbottabad not far from the KFC restaurant where we had had lunch.

The killing of Ben Laden and the drone strikes, considered by many to be a violation of Pakistan's sovereignty, turned a heavy majority of Pakistanis against the United States. A poll by the Gallop organization in early 2013 showed that 92 percent of the Pakistanis surveyed disapproved of U.S. leadership, the lowest in history.

Tensions increased.

The American Embassy in Islamabad continued to issue strong warnings not to travel to Pakistan. *"Due to security concerns,"* one *travel advisory cautioned, "the U.S. Embassy has restricted its employees from going to restaurants and markets in Islamabad April 17 – May 5. We recommend that U.S. citizens in Islamabad during this period take similar precautions. Also, based on current security conditions and a significant increase in the level of sectarian violence in northern Pakistan, the U.S. Embassy has prohibited its employees from taking personal trips to the Gilgit/Skardu area until further notice."*

Elfie and I had hoped to return in September or October. We put off a decision. Conditions in Pakistan were too unstable. The sectarian violence, primarily extremists linked with the Taliban, seemed aimed at destroying Pakistan.

Pakistan seemed to have two choices. It was either to become a land as warlike as the area was in the days of the emperor Aurangzeb in the Seventeenth Century, or its constitutional underpinnings would take hold and true reform would begin.

On May 11, 2013, elections were held. More than 60 percent of eligible voters participated. It was one of the largest turnouts in Pakistan's history. Women were heavily represented.

To lead the country, voters chose Nawaz Sharif, who had been ousted in a military coup by Parvez Musharraf in 1999. Gen. Musharraf had returned to Pakistan a few weeks earlier, hoping to run for office. The Supreme Court put him under house arrest and ruled that he could not run because he had been indicted for complicity in the assassination of Benezir Bhutto.

The election was not without violence. Murders, kidnappings, and bombings marked the days before the voting. But the voters' choice of a civilian government marked the first democratic transition between civilian governments in Pakistan's history. It was an encouraging sign that the people wanted democracy.

Immediately after the election, Sharif said he would build better relations with "our American friends," including "facilitating" withdrawal of American troops from Afghanistan and working to stop the use of drones over Pakistan. He also said "we will take serious measures, as far as law and order is concerned, as far as terrorism or extremism is concerned," and that he would work with the Taliban and "address economic issues very seriously."

He has much to do.

I think often of Javid Iqbal's comment that it would take 200 years to build Pakistan. I wonder if there is time.

What will happen to the people of Pakistan? Earlier, Saleem Malik had offered an answer:

"The Indus Valley and its people are as old as time and we are here to stay," he had told me in Islamabad. "What political dispensation we get remains to be seen. I don't think the madness of a few will matter much in the long run. We have been a bridge between Central Asia and the sea for centuries, and our Sufi tradition is strong. Let us see what happens in the near future."

Acknowledgements

This book owes much to many people. Especially, I want to thank Saeed Anwar Khan and Saleem Akbar Malik, not only for their friendship over many years but for setting up the appointments with what Saeed modestly described as "interesting people."

Those "interesting people" form much of the content of this book and, without boring the reader by repeating their names, I want to thank them all for their interest and for the time they were willing to give Elfie and me. I wish only that we had had more time. There were and are longer discussions I would have like to have had.

Much of my earlier experiences in Pakistan have been left out of the book. Many were fleeting encounters which left indelible memories but did not fit into the present narrative. There was a man I met who had a bullet hole in his ear. "I turned at just the right time," he told me. There was the hotel manager who told me he watched American movies to learn to speak with a generalized American accent. "People pay more attention if they think I'm American, not Pakistani," he explained. And there were many non-Pakistanis. Among them was Isobel Shaw. When her husband Robert, later head of the Aga Khan Foundation, was first posted to

217

Karachi she asked for a guide book. Told none existed, she wrote her own, traveling to barely accessible villages and gathering facts and impressions with wit and insight. There was Margaret Brown, whose late husband, Maj. Willie Brown, played a major role in bringing the northern areas into Pakistan, and who gave me, during conversations in Gilgit and during a long afternoon at her house in the Scottish borders, a feeling for that northwest part of India in the last days of the British Raj.

In America, I want to thank members of the Santa Monica Monthly Meeting of Friends (Quakers) for a small travel grant which helped to pay some of the cost of our air fare and for their interest in this book.

For readers who want to learn more, there are so many books that I would not presume to list them all. They can be found at on-line bookstores or in libraries, and they can provide many hours of enjoyable reading.

The Author

James B. Shuman has been an award-winning newspaper reporter and an editor and writer on the staff of the Reader's Digest. He served, first, in the Digest's Washington, DC office, ghost writing articles for U.S. Senators and members of the House of Representatives, as well as writing under his own by-line. After three years as an editor at the magazine's Pleasantville, NY, headquarters, he returned to writing. He covered, in the United States, a variety of articles ranging from international trade agreements, to the introduction of Supertankers, to Richard Nixon's first trip to Europe as President, to the first three Apollo moon landings, 11, 12, 13. For the Digest's British edition, he wrote on subjects as varied as the British Clean Air Act, the Tate Gallery, and the American Museum at Bath. For the magazine's international editions in Paris, he wrote on such topics as the city of Rotterdam, the international consortium that set up the Airbus Company, and opera star Jessye Norman.

He has been a senior staff associate to John D. Rockefeller 3rd, president of a philanthropic foundation in Pittsburgh, PA, and from 1975 to 1980 an aide to President Gerald R. Ford. In the White House, he designed a daily news summary for the President and White House staff and supervised the office which produced it.

He wrote the President's briefing books for news conferences and interviews and for campaign trips. From 1977 to 1980, he served President Ford in a variety of capacities, traveling with the former President to college campuses across the country, and handling President Ford's logistical arrangements at the 1980 Republican convention.

He has been a consulting editor to the magazine *Business Tokyo*, and has written for a variety of other magazines.

He has co-authored two books: *The Kondratieff Wave* (with David L. Rosenau); World/Times Mirror, (1974), which went through two printings and which landed him a variety of newspaper, radio, and television interviews, including a fifteen minute interview on the Today Show; and *In Constant Fear* (with Peter Remick), Reader's Digest Press (1975).

He and Elfie now live in Northern California.

CPSIA information can be obtained at www.ICGtesting.com
Printed in the USA
LVOW13s1837150714

394459LV00018B/1411/P